Presents

The High School Athlete's Guide to College Baseball

Copyright 2008 by College Bound Sports
All rights reserved.

PUBLISHER
Mazz Marketing
Wayne Mazzoni
287 Courtland Ave.
Black Rock, CT 06605
Phone: 203-260-4932
Fax: 866-209-1305
Email: Wayne@WayneMazzoni.com
Web: www.WayneMazzoni.com

Reproduction of this guide is strictly forbidden!

This guide has been copyrighted with the United States Copyright Office. No part of it may be reproduced in any form or by any electronic or mechanical means, including information storage and retrieval systems, without permission in writing from the publisher, except by a reviewer who may quote brief passages in a review.

ACKNOWLEDGMENTS
We would like to thank all of the college coaches, high school coaches, pro scouts, guidance counselors, and college admissions officers who have contributed information for this guide. Excerpts from US News & World Report articles and NCAA, NAIA, and NJCAA literature are also incorporated.

Every effort has been made to make this guide as accurate as possible. Nevertheless, you should still contact the appropriate college organizations since rules and requirements change frequently. College Bound Sports cannot assume responsibility for any errors contained herein.

WE WANT TO HEAR FROM YOU!
Please e-mail any additions, corrections, ideas, or personal stories you feel would improve this guide to Wayne@WayneMazzoni.com

TESTIMONIALS

"…an extremely valuable tool for high school baseball athletes. I strongly recommend it to any athlete who aspires to play college ball."
Chip Baker, Director of Baseball Operations, Florida State University

"*The Guide To College Baseball* should be a must for every player hoping to move on to college ball or the pros. The recruiting process is overwhelming, confusing, and frustrating for players and their parents. This will help simplify the whole process and answer all of your questions."
Bryan Peters, Hitting Coach, University of South Florida

"This is the best college recruiting guide for baseball that I have seen. It is thorough, the information is complete and it brings you through the college admission and recruiting process step by step. You will not find a more informative guide to help you through this difficult process."
Kendall Baker, Counselor, AD & Head Coach, Perkiomen School (PA)

"The information in *The Guide To College Baseball* is right on target! It will save time and could be worth thousands of dollars to the prospective college baseball player. I highly recommend it."
Jim Grief, Pro Scout, Cincinnati Reds

"There is not a better recruiting guide for high school baseball players in the country! The time and effort that went into this guide is matched only by its thoroughness and attention to detail."
Bill Hamilton, Head Coach, Pensacola Community College (FL)

"I believe wholeheartedly that *The Guide To College Baseball* will help you tremendously with your college search."
Dan Callahan, Head Coach, Southern Illinois University

"This guide gives you the opportunity to choose the correct school to fit all your needs, so when your athletic career is over, you are well prepared to lead a productive life."
Raphael Cerrato, Recruiting Coordinator, Brown University (RI)

"This is a well thought out, easy-to-read guide to the ins and outs of today's recruiting process."
Rob Penders, Asst. Coach, University of Texas

"This guide informs players and parents of the true realities involved in the lengthy and often frustrating process of preparing a high school athlete to play at the next level. It is a must-read!"
Todd Hode, Asst. Coach, Purdue University (IN)

"This guide includes all the intangible that recruiters look for. If you are committed to take your game to a higher level, it may well be the most important piece of equipment you own!"
Derek Johnson, Pitching Coach, Vanderbilt University (TN)

"A remarkably well-written guide. It is complete, concise, and it is a quick and accurate reference source for any athlete...one of the best guides I have seen."
Brian Thomas, Head Coach, Ursinus College (PA)

Copyright 2008 Mazz Marketing   203--260-4932   Wayne@WayneMazzoni.com

We would like to thank the following people in the sports community for contributing valuable information to the guide and supporting our effort to help high school athletes navigate the college recruiting maze.

Organization	Advisor	Current or Former Title
AKADEMA BASEBALL GLOVES (NJ)	Joe Gilligan, Jr.	CEO
ANNA JONESBORO HIGH SCHOOL (IL)	Rick Bittle	Head Coach
BASEBALL FACTORY (MD)	Steve Sclafani	CEO
BENEDICTINE HIGH SCHOOL (OH)	Brian Sliwinski	Head Coach
BROWN UNIVERSITY (RI)	Raphael Cerrato	Recruiting Coordinator
C.J. STEWART BASEBALL SCHOOL	C.J. Stewart	Executive Director
CALVIN COLLEGE (MI)	Gary West	Assistant Coach
CINCINNATI REDS	Jim Grief	Pro Scout
CLEVELAND INDIANS	Vic Power	Former 7x All-Star 1B
COAST TO COAST ATHLETICS (OH)	Kevin Ritter	Executive Director
COCOA EXPO SPORTS CENTER (FL)	Jeff Biddle	Director of Athletics
COLLEGE OF CHARLESTON (SC)	Gregg Mucerino	Assistant Coach
COLLEGE OF NEW JERSEY	Dean Glus	Assistant Coach
DECKER SPORTS USA (NE)	Thomas Decker	President
ELMHURST COLLEGE (IL)	Clark Jones	Head Coach
ELON COLLEGE (NC)	Mike Kennedy	Head Coach
FLORIDA ATLANTIC UNIVERSITY	Bob Deutschman	Assistant Coach
FLORIDA STATE UNIVERSITY	Chip Baker	Assistant Coach
FOCUSED BASEBALL (FL)	Tom Hansen, PhD.	President
FROZEN ROPES TRAINING CENTER (NY)	Tony Abbatine	President
GLOUCESTER COUNTY COLLEGE (NJ)	Rob Valli	Head Coach
GREENSBORO COLLEGE (NC)	Scott Rash	Former Head Coach
HIGH SCHOOL SPORTS SHOW NETWORK (PA)	Adam Stanco	Producer & Host
HOFSTRA UNIVERSITY (NY)	Mike Reid	Assistant Coach
HOPE COLLEGE (MI)	Stu Fritz	Head Coach
JOE ESPINOSA BASEBALL SCHOOL (CT)	Joe Espinosa	President
LOUISIANA STATE UNIVERSITY	Bob Smith	Former Assistant Coach
MIAMI UNIVERSITY (OH)	Bill Consiglio	Assistant Coach
MICKEY OWEN BASEBALL SCHOOL (MO)	Ken Rizzo	Director
MIKE EPSTEIN HITTING (CA)	Mike Epstein	President & former MLB player
MORRIS BROWN COLLEGE (GA)	Marqus Johnson	Assistant Coach
NEDCO SPORTS (AL)	Nick Dixon	Head Coach
OCEAN TOWNSHIP HIGH SCHOOL (NJ)	Del Dal Pra	Head Coach
PADUCAH COMMUNITY COLLEGE (KY)	Rick Tippin	Former Head Coach
PENSACOLA JUNIOR COLLEGE (FL)	Bill Hamilton	Head Coach
PERKIOMEN SCHOOL (PA)	Kendall Baker	AD & Head Coach
PRESBYTERIAN UNIVERSITY (SC)	Jeremy Farber	Assistant Coach
PUERTO RICO BASEBALL ACADEMY	Edwin Correa	President & Former MLB player
SACRED HEART UNIVERSITY (CT)	Seth Kaplan	Assistant Coach
SOUTH GEORGIA COLLEGE	Zach Walker	Assistant Coach
SOUTHERN ILLINOIS UNIVERSITY	Dan Callahan	Head Coach
SPRINGFIELD COLLEGE (IL)	Steve Torricelli	AD & Head Coach
ST. THOMAS UNIVERSITY (FL)	Manny Mantrana	Head Coach
ST. THOMAS UNIVERSITY (FL)	Garrett Quinn	Pitching Coach
SAN JACINTO COLLEGE (TX)	Rob Penders	Assistant Coach
SHO-ME BASEBALL CAMP (MO)	Chris Schroeder	Director
SOUTHWEST HIGH SCHOOL (FL)	Javier Perez	Head Coach
STANFORD UNIVERSITY (CA)	Dean Stotz	Associate Head Coach
TENNESSE TECH UNIVERSITY	Pat Portugal	Former Assistant Coach
TEXAS A & M UNIVERSITY	Jorge Hernandez	Assistant Head Coach
TODAYS MVP.COM (NJ)	Lou Santangelo	CEO
UNIVERSITY OF ALABAMA	Bobby Pierce	Head Coach
UNIVERSITY OF CONNECTICUT	Jim Penders	Assistant Coach
UNIVERSITY OF EVANSVILLE (IL)	Jim Brownlee	Head Coach
UNIVERSITY OF LOUISVILLE (KY)	Al Lopez	Former Assistant Coach
UNIVERSITY OF NEBRASKA	Ron Wolforth	Former Assistant Coach
UNIVERSITY OF NORTHERN COLORADO	Terry Hensley	Head Coach
UNIVERSITY OF SOUTH FLORIDA	Bryan Peters	Hitting Coach
UNIVERSITY OF SOUTHERN MISSISSIPPI	Clay Smith	Assistant Coach
USSSA	Chet Kapla	Showcase Director
VANDERBILT UNIVERSITY (TN)	Derek Johnson	Pitching Coach
WEST CHESTER UNIVERSITY (PA)	Chris Calciano	Head Coach

TABLE OF CONTENTS

INTRODUCTION... 7

1. MASTER THE RECRUITING PROCESS
How a College Coach Thinks About Recruiting........................... 11
15 Pitfalls to Avoid.. 16

2. ENERGIZE YOUR SUPPORT GROUP
Parents.. 23
Guidance Counselor... 28
High School Coach... 31

3. HOW TO IMPROVE YOUR PROFILE
Baseball Suggestions.. 34
Academic Suggestions.. 42

4. YOUR COLLEGE LINE-UP
Creating Your Target List.. 48

5. ESSENTIAL ACTION STEPS TO TAKE
Promoting Yourself... 62
Going on Campus Visits... 67
Hiring Recruiting Services.. 71
Trying to Make the Team as a Walk-on................................... 73
Attending Showcases.. 74
Producing a Highlight Video.. 81
Travel, All-Star & Select Teams... 85

6. DRIVE DOWN THE COST OF COLLEGE
Facts About Financial Aid.. 88
What You Need To Know About Loans................................... 91
Tips for Receiving the Best Package.. 93
Financial Aid Timeline... 98
Serve Your Country & Get a Great Education........................ 99

7. THE COLLEGE LANDSCAPE BY DIVISION
NCAA... 103
- Division I... 104
- Division II.. 106
- Division III... 107
NAIA.. 108
NJCAA... 109

8. FORMS YOU'LL NEED & REFERENCES YOU'LL USE
Checklist... 112

Correspondence.. 115
Internet Sites.. 120
Online College Questionnaire.. 124
College Information Sheet.. 125
Identify Your #1 Choice.. 127
Cost of College Comparison... 128
Estimated Family Contribution... 129

GLOSSARY OF TERMS 131

INTERNATIONAL STUDENTS 139

REVIEW
10 Things to Remember During the Recruiting Process.. 140

HOW DID WE DO? 141

INTRODUCTION

Congratulations!
By reading this guide, you are giving yourself an enormous advantage over your competitors-thousands of other high school athletes your age who also want to play college baseball.

Gaining admission to the college of your choice can be a daunting experience for the average high school student. The task is even more intricate for baseball players. Success requires a solid plan, attention to detail, and disciplined execution. Unfortunately, many high school athletes looking to continue competing in college do not have a true understanding of how the recruiting process works, and never reach their athletic or academic potential.

This book provides a roadmap for you to follow when making the jump from high school to college baseball. If you avoid the mistakes most high school players make, promote yourself aggressively, and improve your athletic and academic skills, we are confident you will find a school that is right for you!

What We Want To Accomplish
Our goal is to help you find a college where you will be able to:
- Receive a quality education to prepare you for life after college, whether or not it includes baseball.
- Compete on a college baseball team and have a chance to be an everyday player.
- Possibly earn an athletic and/or academic scholarship.
- Obtain the best financial aid package to lower the expenses of college for you and your family.
- Feel confident in your ultimate college selection, reducing the chance of transferring or dropping out.

A Big Decision
We hope you're excited about the opportunity that awaits you: the chance to attend college and continue your baseball career. College promises to be one of the most enjoyable, rewarding, and memorable times of your life. We want to make sure you select a school that meets all of your needs.

Choosing which school to attend is a big decision. College is where you will develop many of your lifelong friends; it can determine where you eventually live, what livelihood you choose after baseball, and the possibility of a professional baseball career. It's even where you may meet your future husband or wife.

So, devote whatever time and energy you need from now until the end of your senior year to make sure you promote yourself in an intelligent and informative way. Although your parents, coaches, and teachers can help, your future rests in your hands. Are you motivated and determined enough to do the required work? We hope so, because the results of your efforts could pay dividends the rest of your life.

Think of the process as a job search. If you were looking for employment, would you wait for companies to call you? Of course not! You would be proactive and let companies know that you want to be hired. That's what you need to do here.

Start Early
Don't wait until your senior year to begin your college search. As you will learn in this Guide, finding the right school for you requires a continuous effort over an extended period of time. We recommend you begin your search once you enter high school. If you are currently a junior or senior, your effort will need to be more intense and focused.

Maintain a Positive Attitude

Unfortunately, the college recruiting and search process can be filled with disappointments: you don't perform well in a big game or at a baseball showcase; you don't have the statistics you hoped for; you learn that your top school doesn't need a player at your position; you don't make the All-League team as you had expected; or no school offers you a scholarship. Whatever roadblocks you face, do your best not to get discouraged. Try to maintain a positive and upbeat attitude and have confidence that you will ultimately reach your goal. Confidence is an important key to success in life, as well as on the diamond.

Assumptions

If you are reading this guide, we assume you would like to gain a better understanding of the college recruiting process. You probably feel confused and are unsure what steps you should take to attract the attention of college recruiters. Most of your anxiety can be avoided if you are aware of the recruiting process. That's where we can help.

This guide is loaded with useful information to give you the confidence and skills you need to market yourself and give you a better chance to identify and attend the school of your dreams.

We're also assuming that few coaches outside of your local area know your name, even if you're an outstanding ballplayer with tons of potential. It's no secret that college coaches from the top programs first recruit in talent-rich baseball cities like Miami, Los Angeles, Atlanta, Dallas, and Tampa. Players from these warm-weather climates have the advantage of competing year-round, generally making them more skilled and experienced athletes. Although you may be at a disadvantage because of where you live geographically, don't be discouraged. We're going to show you how to generate attention from coaches all around the country, whether you live in sunny San Diego, California or chilly Bangor, Maine.

Get Your Degree

There are countless stories of high school players who seek lucrative major league contracts but never get them. Only one out of every 250,000 high school players will ever compete in the big leagues. We hope you're one of them, but we also want you to realize you have a much better chance of becoming a successful businessperson, doctor or lawyer, if you graduate from college first. Once you receive a college degree, no one can ever take it away from you. It can help lead the way to financial security for the rest of your life.

This guide is written for high school athletes who want to play collegiate baseball and receive a college degree. It is not for the student who only wants to play pro baseball and has no interest in furthering his education. This is guide is also not written for blue chip players who receive national publicity, genuine interest from pro scouts, and invitations to the country's top showcases.

Let Others Help You

It is important that you share this guide and advice with your parents, coaches, guidance counselors, and any other people assisting you with your college search. You will benefit immensely from the opinions and experiences of people who have your best interests at heart and have been down this road before.

Why We Wrote This Guide

Since 1991, our company has organized camps, showcases, and tournaments for more than 7,000 high school players. Even though most of these top athletes aspired to compete at the college level, few of them got the chance and their careers ended prematurely. We couldn't understand why this was happening so we decided to learn everything we could about the college recruiting process.

The information we've compiled during the last 16 years features extensive research with hundreds of college coaches, guidance counselors, high school players, parents, and pro scouts.

Here's What We've Concluded:

The main reason so many talented student-athletes never realize their dreams of competing in college is because:

- They don't understand the recruiting process.
- They don't apply to appropriate schools.
- They don't prepare academically and athletically.
- They don't promote themselves properly.

We don't want this to happen to you!

With 1,343 college baseball programs in the United States, we know there is a school out there that needs an player just like you. Now, let's go find it!

1
MASTER THE RECRUITING PROCESS

In This Chapter

- How college coaches recruit
- Where they go to find their players
- A college coach's "A-list"
- When the peak recruiting season is
- The kinds of background checks coaches do
- How a coach expresses interest in a recruit
- Some basic facts about scholarships
- Pitfalls to avoid in the recruiting process

This chapter covers the basic-and not-so-basic-information about the recruiting process. By the end of this chapter, you should have a better understanding of how it all works.

HOW A COLLEGE COACH THINKS ABOUT RECRUITING

You will have an enormous advantage over your competition if you are familiar with the recruiting process from a college coach's standpoint. Not every college recruits exactly as described below-coaches at smaller schools have less money to recruit and may travel less than their Division I counterpart, for example - but the information below is typical of most baseball programs.

A Coach Is Always Looking For Top Athletes

A coach constantly keeps his ears and eyes open for players who can help his team. Naturally, he will spend the majority of his time focusing on his next recruiting class. However, if you are a talented underclassman and you impressed a college coach, either at a camp, a game, a tournament, or from a newspaper article he read about you, he will probably keep your name in his recruiting database and follow your development.

"I try to determine what the recruit is going to be like in two or three years. Does he have the potential to work hard and become better? Is his speed and power there? Basically, I look for everything a major league scout would look for with the #1 pick." - Jeff Albies, William Patterson University, Head Baseball Coach, NCAA D-III

Coaches Help Each Other Recruit

College coaches belong to a small fraternity. Nationwide, there are only 1,343 head coaches and a few thousand assistants. Many are good friends, work the same summer camps, and socialize at the American Baseball Coaches Association's annual convention. Also, many coaches change jobs frequently and devote a lot of time maintaining their professional network of contacts. On occasion, they even share information about top athletes and assist each other with recruiting (assuming they are not rivals in the same conference).

Few college coaches can recruit every outstanding athlete he or his staff sees. If a desirable athlete's grades don't meet his school's requirements, or the athlete is a shortstop and the coach is already stocked with quality shortstops, the coach may recommend the athlete to other coaches he knows.

That's why it's important to develop relationships with as many coaches as you can. If a summer camp coach is really impressed with you, make an effort to stay in touch with him via mail or e-mail. Update him on your development. Even if he doesn't coach at a school that interests you, he could be your ticket to a college scholarship somewhere else. Remember, it's not who you know, but who knows you!

State Schools Like to Recruit Locally

For the most part, public school coaches concentrate on players who live within their home state. Since state governments fund public universities, they have a responsibility to provide opportunities first and foremost for in-state students. Also, since tuition is often much cheaper for in-state students, it is more cost-effective for coaches to offer scholarships to in-state athletes. With this in mind, you may want to take a close look at the public schools in your home state.

"I try to identify the best possible talent out there. Being a state school, we do most of our recruiting in the New Jersey area because it's the most cost effective for the kids and their parents" - Jeff Albies, William Patterson University, Head Baseball Coach, NCAA D-III

Developing an "A-list"

When the recruiting process usually begins in the spring of each year. Coaching staffs assemble an "A-list" of high school juniors they are interested in recruiting. The list will typically include several high school and junior college players at each position where there is a need. The names on this list are players the coaches have seen in action at a camp, showcase, tournament, or high school or summer league game. They also come from referrals by trusted sources like other college coaches, boosters, former athletes, sports reporters, pro scouts, credible recruiting services, and some high school coaches. Many junior college coaches also keep an eye out for "late developing" seniors.

It is important to remember that their "A-lists" are composed of high school juniors-to-be, meaning they appeared on their radar long before their junior year. With this in mind, place yourself in position to be noticed and/or evaluated by recruiters before your junior year.

This can be accomplished by: playing for prominent league teams outside of school; participating in college camps held by the schools you are interested in; attending showcase camps college coaches attend; and, personally notifying the coach of your interest in his program and letting him know your qualifications.

Determining Who Is Interested

Questionnaires are sent to every player on a coach's "A-list," as well as to any player who writes or phones the coach's office expressing interest in the program. If you receive a questionnaire, you will be asked to provide detailed academic and athletic information about yourself and to return the form promptly. If you neglect to return it quickly, be aware that you are sending a strong message that you are not interested in being recruited. Some elite athletes on the "A-list" who do not return their questionnaires may receive a follow-up phone call to determine their interest level, but most will not.

Returning the questionnaire promptly does more than tell the coach you are interested in his program. It also tells him you are conscientious, able to follow instructions and pay attention to detail. Sometimes, little things like that can make all the difference in the world. While you may not stand out from the crowd by doing this, you'll definitely stand out if your questionnaire comes in late, is completed in a sloppy fashion or lacks important information.

Peak Recruiting Season

Once the college academic year ends, usually in late May to early June, most of the coaches on staff fan out to attend hundreds of high school games, tournaments, summer league games, and showcases. (At NCAA D-I schools, three coaches are allowed to recruit, but only two can be on the road at one time.) Their goal is to personally scot as many players on their "A-list" as possible, as well as find any new talent they may have overlooked. Their "A-list' will constantly change as players who impress the coaches over the summer are added and others who don't perform well or show no interest are removed. Some will also be removed for poor grades or low SAT/ACT scores, and for disciplinary reasons.

Working With Admissions Officers to Narrow Down the List

Coaches meet periodically with their college's admissions officer liaison to discuss prospective recruits. This is where your ability on the field can help you get admitted to a good academic school you might not qualify for on grades or test scores alone. A coach will compile a list of his top recruits so the liaison knows which athletes are the coach's highest priorities.

Based on your academic credentials, the liaison will often tell the coach who has a chance to be admitted and who does not. Some admission departments will be flexible and accept top recruits who may fall slightly below the academic requirements, but this happens only if you are in high demand by the coaching staff.

In the fall, the coaching staff will then begin to reduce their "A-list" to a more manageable and realistic pool of candidates. It will only contain students who can contribute athletically, fill a position need on the team, and possess the academic marks to get accepted to the school.

In-Home Visits
Some coaches will visit top recruits in their homes. If a head coach or assistant coach comes to your house, he will want to meet with you, your parents, and maybe your high school coach. The coach's goal is to explain the benefits of his school's academic program and baseball team, discuss scholarships and financial aid, and determine your interest level in his school. Obviously, he also wants to get to know you as a person and make sure he is making a wise investment of his time, coaching resources, and, possibly, scholarship funds.

NCAA Clearinghouse
A NCAA member coach will require confirmation from the Clearinghouse that you are academically eligible to compete in college baseball. If you have not achieved the required grades, test scores, and taken the right courses, the coach will immediately eliminate you from his recruiting list. Don't get knocked out of the recruiting game before it even starts by under achieving in class. See Chapter 7 for more information on the Clearinghouse.

Core Courses
The NCAA requires a certain number of college preparatory (core) courses to be completed in high school before an athlete is eligible to play his or her freshman year. This requirement recently changed from 13 to 14 and it's possible it may change again.

Make sure in your freshman year you know the current requirement for your graduating class and are taking enough core courses to qualify. If athletes have insufficient core courses when they graduate, they not only won't be allowed to play baseball during their freshman year of college, they also won't be allowed to receive an athletic scholarship.

Players who fail to complete the required number of core courses will be allowed to play beginning with their sophomore year and also to receive a scholarship, but the sad truth is that that year of inactivity may cost them a valuable scholarship as the coach may opt for another player.

Coaches Do Their Homework, Too
Before a coach decides to offer you a scholarship, he will do an extensive background check to find out everything he can about you. A scholarship is a big financial risk, but if a coach is very thorough in his research, he improves the chances of making an intelligent decision. A few phone calls to your high school coach, guidance counselor, teachers, summer league coach, friends, and any local contacts he has will provide the information he needs.

So ask yourself right now:
- Is there anything I am doing now that will negatively affect a college coach's opinion of me?
- Do I attend all of my classes?
- Do I get along with my teammates?
- Am I a leader or a follower?
- What kind of crowd do I hang out with?
- How is my work ethic, drive, and integrity?

Scholarships & Walk-Ons
Once the baseball staff has finalized its recruiting list, it's time to decide which incoming freshmen or transfer students will receive baseball scholarships and how much money each person will receive. All other players on

their recruiting list will be invited to try to make the team as a walk-on, assuming they still want to attend the school.

Telephone Calls
College coaches are not allowed to call you until July 1 before the start of your senior year. You are permitted to call a college coach as often as you like, but do not abuse this privilege and acquire the dreaded "nuisance" tag. After July 1, a coach is limited to one outgoing phone call to you per week, except during these situations:
- 5 days before your official campus visit.
- On the day of a coach's off-campus visit with you.
- On the initial date for signing the National Letter of Intent and two days after that.

Letter of Intent
At the NCAA D-I level, there is an early signing period in mid-November and a late signing period in mid-April where a coach will try to persuade his top recruits who have been offered athletic scholarships to sign a National Letter of Intent. This letter is a binding contract that guarantees the recruit will enroll at their school.

 NCAA D-I and D-II schools must wait until September 1 of your junior year before sending you promotional items like school or team publications, media guides, and playing schedules.

Facts About Scholarships
The number of full baseball scholarships that each school can distribute is strictly limited. Here are the maximum allotments, even though many schools are limited to far less either by their conference or their own administration's limitations

Division	Full Scholarships	Division	Full Scholarships
NCAA D-I	11.7	NAIA	12
NCAA D-I Ivy & Patriot Leagues	0	NJCAA D-I	24
NCAA D-II	9	NJCAA D-II	24
NCAA D-III	0	NJCAA D-III	0

Each coach decides how to award his scholarship allotment. It makes the most sense to divide the allotment into several partial scholarships as opposed to giving only a few players full scholarships. It's a lower risk strategy because some of the scholarship recipients will fall short of expectations, get injured, become academically ineligible, or drop out.

Also, realize that the scholarships are not just earmarked for incoming freshmen, but are used for all athletes on the team. This may include as many as 35 sophomores, juniors, seniors, and fifth-year athletes. As a result, thousands of outstanding high school players are never offered even partial scholarships. Many don't even receive passing interest from coaches. Keep in mind that scholarship awards are on a year-to-year basis. While a coach cannot guarantee you will receive the same award in future years, it is normal practice that it will be renewed at the same level.

Even if you are fortunate enough to get all or some of your tuition paid for with an athletic scholarship, you may still have other significant costs like room and board, books, entertainment, and transportation to and from school. D-III and D-I Ivy League and Patriot League schools do not offer any athletic scholarships (American University, a Patriot League member is the exception). Military academies like Air Force, West Point, Navy, and the Coast Guard are tuition-free; however admission requires a congressional recommendation.

In addition to allocating scholarships, a coach can consult with financial aid officers on your behalf to determine what non-athletic aid might be available. However, you should personally check out for yourself other areas of help since you cannot expect the coach to explore all available options for each prospect.

Likely Letters

If you are offered a baseball scholarship, you must inform the college in either November or April if you are going to accept it. Since you will not hear from the admission or financial aid office until mid-April that you have been accepted to the school and offered a financial aid package, you will receive a "Likely Letter."

This states whether you are likely or unlikely to be accepted to the school and receive a financial aid package. The "Likely Letter" allows you to make an informed decision about where to go to school, without forcing you to void the scholarship.

One Athlete's Lost Opportunity
Louis Medina, 25 years old, Brooklyn, NY

As an All-Country second baseman for my high school team, I led the league in batting average. I was convinced a college coach would offer me a baseball scholarship. I worked hard on the field and always strived to improve my performance. I went to camps, played on an American Legion summer ball team, and took private lessons.

But there's one thing I forgot to do -- inform college coaches that I wanted to be recruited. I just assumed they would come to me and that my stats would speak for themselves. No one told me I had to take the initiative and write letters, send highlight tapes, and attend showcases. I was so wrong and as a result, I had to hang up my spikes at age 18 when I headed off to college.

As I look back on my college days, I'm thankful for the great education I received, the friends I made, and the way school prepared me for a rewarding career. Yet, there's one thing I definitely would have really enjoyed -- the opportunity to play college baseball. I'm confident that I could have contributed somewhere, possibly a small to midsize northern college. If I had only aggressively promoted myself in high school, I'm sure I would have had more options and a much more rewarding college experience.

15 PITFALLS TO AVOID

Most high school players never get the opportunity to suit up in a college uniform. It's important for you to understand the main reasons why this happens. Avoid their mistakes and you will substantially improve your chances of playing college ball.

1. I Only Want To Compete For A High-Profile NCAA D-I Team.

If you only focus your search on the country's top baseball teams, you will be disappointed. Too many high school athletes think that programs like Miami, Stanford, Florida State, Louisiana State, Texas, and other high-profile schools are the only respectable ones in the country.

While many high school athletes dream of one day competing on ESPN in a packed stadium at the College World Series, in reality, very few get the opportunity. According to our research, roughly two percent of all high school and junior college athletes who seek to compete at a D-I school will ever get the chance.

If you're just finishing your junior year of high school, you'll have a pretty good idea if you are talented enough to compete at that level. Blue chip athletes recruited by these nationally ranked schools are often:
- Three or four-year varsity starters for their high school teams
- All-State or All-County award recipients
- Receive recruiting calls and letters from numerous coaches
- Attract many college coaches and pro scouts at their games
- Invited to prestigious tournaments like Team One's National Showcase

Think you need to attend a high-profile NCAA D-I School to play pro sports? Check out where these famous players attended college:

MLB Player	College	MLB Player	College
Ben Sheets	NE Louisiana	Joe Nathan	Stony Brook
B.J. Ryan	SW Louisiana	Mike Piazza	Miami-Dade
Billy Wagner	Ferrum	Ellis Burks	Ranger Junior College
Jeff Francis	Lethbridge	Jeff Bagwell	University of Hartford
Moises Alou	Canada College	Tim Salmon	Grand Canyon College
Chuck Finley	NE Louisiana St	Jim Thome	Illinois Central College
Roy Oswalt	Holmes	Curt Schilling	Yavapai Junior College

LESSON LEARNED: If you are not a "blue-chip" recruit, expand your college search and include a wide range of schools on your target list.

"Sometimes, the shoe doesn't fit, that's all. High school players today turn on the TV in June and see the College World Series and that's all they focus on. Meanwhile, they are light years away from that level. They have to do what's in their reach." - Jeff Albies, Head Baseball Coach, William Patterson University, NCAA D-III

2. I Must Be A Hot Recruit. Coaches Send Me Letters All the Time.

Do not assume form letters in your mailbox mean that a coach considers you a prospect. Every high school player who expresses interest in a college team, regardless of his ability, will receive a letter and questionnaire

in the mail asking for more information. In fact, some D-I schools may send out as many as 10,000 letters each year! Understand that this is only an initial request for information and, in most cases, an expected courtesy. Answer the following questions honestly:
- Do college coaches call me?
- Is my mailbox overflowing with letters from coaches who want me to consider their schools?
- Are coaches coming to my house to meet with my parents and me?
- Do recruiters and pro scouts travel specifically to watch my games?
- Am I receiving all-expense paid invitations to campuses?

If you're one of the lucky few who can answer "yes" to some of the above questions, then consider yourself a blue-chip prospect. If you're like most high school athletes, however, and you had to answer "no" to all or most of the questions, then you need to take a pro-active approach to your college search.

LESSON LEARNED: Receiving phone calls, personalized hand-written letters from college coaches, and requests for personal meetings is a much better indicator-rather than form letters and questionnaires-of how interested a coach is in recruiting you.

3. I'll Make the College Team as a Walk-On.
If you only receive lukewarm interest from coaches, but you really want to play college ball, you can try making the team as a "walk-on." This means you participate in an open tryout when you arrive in the fall.

However, understand that it may be difficult to make the team as a non-recruited athlete. Your odds of success are not high. The tryouts are usually brief -- most players get cut after the first day -- and as many as 100 players can show up. Every now and then a coach may find a "diamond in the rough," like a hard-throwing pitcher, who has gone unnoticed. For the most part, however, a coach knows exactly which players will comprise his squad before the open tryout even begins. This is another reason why failing to match your actual skill level with the competitive skill level of the school you are trying to compete at is a bad mistake.

LESSON LEARNED: Even if you make the team, you may have a slim chance of ever playing in a game. You may want to search harder for a school that wants you and that you fit with talent-wise. Many athletes who try to "walk-on," not including "recruited walk-ons" who we will discuss in Chapter 5, do not make the team and transfer or drop out after their freshman year. Check out our "Hit the Web" section in Chapter 4 for the best way to search for schools that fit your talent level.

"We have a good walk-on program, but there is very little chance for someone to make an impact that way. We don't give them the opportunity to. We don't have a JV program here and we have a pretty good idea from the start of who will make an impact." - Mike Martin, Head Baseball Coach, Florida State University, NCAA D-I

4. My High School Coach Is Going To Get Me A Scholarship.
Do not rely on your high school coach to contact college coaches, write letters, or solicit offers on your behalf. Most high school coaches are unable or unwilling to devote the large amounts of time required to help their players find the right college. If your coach has time to assist you with the recruiting process and has demonstrated a commitment to help you find a school that meets your needs, consider yourself lucky.

Too frequently, we hear from parents that their child's high school coach doesn't do anything to help. Often these complaints come in the spring of a high school athlete's senior year, after most college application deadlines have already passed. Don't worry if your coach only limits his involvement to practices and games. Some coaches, for whatever reason, do not feel college recruiting is part of their job responsibility. Some are simply too busy to help. Others are unfamiliar with the recruiting process and might not even know where to begin. Many coaches who sincerely want to help are restricted in their efforts simply because they don't have that many college contacts, except perhaps locally and/or at the college they themselves attended. While thankfully rare, there occasionally exists a coach who is vindictive for one reason or another simply because of a personality conflict!

While this is indeed rare, cases like this have happened. Just another reason high school athletes need to take the initiative and take charge of their own recruiting processes. Some coaches devote all of their time to the "star athlete," because he's the easiest one to promote. Remember: what's on the line in the recruiting game is your future, not your coaches. Don't sit back and wait for someone to help you.

LESSON LEARNED: Don't expect your high school coach to devote much time and effort to personally assist you with your college search. Ask him to help, but take responsibility and control your own future

5. I'd Be Happy Just to Make the Team.

Always set high goals for yourself. We have found that the players who have the best college experience are the ones who make their team's starting lineup. Riding the bench is no fun unless you have the potential to work your way into a more important role within a short period of time. Where would you be happier: Being the 34th out of 35 players on a big school's depth chart and getting a couple of innings during your entire four-year career, or being the star of your team at a small, lesser-known school?

LESSON LEARNED: Find a team where you can contribute and have a realistic chance to start.

6. Lots Of College Coaches Will Watch My High School Games.

If more than a handful of college coaches ever watch you play throughout your high school career, you are in a select group. Even if coaches attend your games, they most likely represent only nearby schools.

Most baseball recruiting budgets do not allow coaches to travel around the country scouting talent. It's just too expensive. Coaches will scout regional high school and summer league games, usually within a couple hours of their school, but rarely will they travel farther. It's just not financially feasible or an efficient use of their time.

It's not unusual for a college coach to spend the majority of his travel and recruiting budget scouting a select few blue-chip prospects. What's left in the travel budget will be used to attend high-profile tournaments and national showcases where the greatest number of prospects can be seen in one place.

Say for example you live in Minnesota and are interested in attending a college in Texas. Even if the coach in Texas really likes you, he probably won't have the money or the time to fly to Minnesota to watch you play. He would rather find out if you are going to attend any showcases or national tournaments where he can see you and a number of other players on his list. Or, he may invite you to attend one of his summer camps.

LESSON LEARNED: Be pro-active and take your skills to coaches of the schools that interest you. Don't expect them to travel to your hometown.

7. Small Colleges Have Weak Teams.

Most athletes believe the misconception that NCAA D-I is the only way to go and that all other college divisions are inferior. Don't fall into this trap! If you do, you will eliminate hundreds of great schools that may need a player just like you.

LESSON LEARNED: Surprisingly, many D-II, D-III, NAIA, and junior college teams stack up well against D-I schools. Don't neglect them simply because of their affiliation.

8. I Want to Play Pro Ball and I Plan to Get Drafted Right Out of High School

If your ultimate goal is to play major-league baseball, keep in mind that you have a much better chance of getting drafted out of college than out of high school. Many pro scouts look favorably upon college graduates because they have had an extra four years or more to develop their abilities. In addition, they are generally more mature, responsible, and less of a financial risk than their younger high school counterparts.

LESSON LEARNED: Go to college and get your degree. It will give you a better chance to make it to the pros.

9. My Stats Are So Impressive That College Coaches Will Come Knocking on My Door With Scholarship Offers

Contrary to popular belief, a high batting average or impressive won-loss pitching record is not enough to attract a recruiter's attention. Here's why coaches feel this way: stats are a direct result of the competition you play against. Coaches are more interested in your skills than mere statistics. When coaches evaluate you, they are projecting where you will be in two or three years at their competitive levels.

They're looking at your bat speed, agility, arm strength, hand and foot speed, hustle, and overall athleticism. Sure, it helps to have impressive states because it leads to publicity and recognition, but coaches don't rely exclusively on these numbers. It wouldn't be unusual, for example, if the best pitcher on a weak high school team in New York was cut from a strong high school team in Florida.

LESSON LEARNED: Stats are only a small part of how a college coach will evaluate you.

There's another reason that college coaches don't rely too heavily on a player's high school stats. They realize that high school scorekeepers can often inflate a player's stats by awarding hits when the fielders should have been charged with errors, and vice-versa.

10. I'm Only Considering Schools Where I Can Earn A Full Ride.

Full-ride scholarships are not as readily available as most players and parents think. A full baseball scholarship is so rare that it almost does not exist. Over 90 percent of all scholarships are awarded to pitchers and most of that money is divided into partial scholarships.

LESSON LEARNED: Don't expect that an athletic scholarship will allow you to attend school for free. Even if you are one of the fortunate few to receive an athletic scholarship, you will probably still have to pay for other college expenses with family money, an academic scholarship, or loans.

11. I'm Only Applying to My First-Choice School. It's the Only Place I Want to Attend.

Even if your heart is set on attending one particular school and the coach has expressed interest in you, you should still promote yourself to other schools. It will give you leverage when it comes time to discuss academic and athletic scholarships, or financial assistance, with the coach and admissions office.

The coach at your first choice school has all the bargaining power if he finds out that you are desperate to attend his school. Plus, you might find that a different school-one you might not have thought of before-is a better fit for you.

LESSON LEARNED: Leverage is crucial if you want to increase your worth and potentially attain a better scholarship. Avoid the temptation to prematurely tell a coach that you've made your decision to attend his school.

> "Very few kids get to play for the school of their choice. That's just the way it is. It's a pretty tough thing to do. They dream about it all their lives and then when they're eligibly recruits, that school isn't interested in them. Then, some other school comes along that shows some interest and then that becomes their top choice. It's funny sometimes how that works out." - Mike Martin, Head Baseball Coach, Florida State University, NCAA D-I

12. I'm Regularly Told by High School, Summer League Coaches, and Scouts that I have the Ability to Play College or Pro Ball.

Constant praise from influential people in the baseball community is nice to hear, but it can also be dangerous. It may cause you to sit back, wait for coaches to come to you, and not be aggressive in your search.

LESSON LEARNED: Always strive to improve your skills. Never stop learning. And, as they say in the business world, don't believe your own PR!

13. If a Coach from a School outside My Target List Wants to Recruit Me, I'll Tell Him I'm Not Interested.

Avoid rushing to judgment if a coach expresses interest in recruiting you. A lot can change in a few months. A school that you dismiss now may look a lot more attractive later on. Never lie to or mislead a coach, make snap judgments. Make sure you research every opportunity before making up your mind.

Once you decide exactly where you want to go, and after you have signed a Letter of Intent, tell the other coaches who are interested in you to remove you from their recruiting list. Make sure to thank them sincerely for their interest in you. Not only does it show good character, but if you ever want to transfer, that school can still be a good option.

LESSON LEARNED: Keep your options open! Avoid rushing to judgment until you have made up your mind. You should also visit each school that shows interest in you-it's the best way to decide if it's a place you not only play baseball for, but make your new home as well.

14. Coaches Will Notice Me When I Have A Big Senior Season.

Unfortunately, by the time your senior season is underway in April, you will probably already know where you are going to college. Also, some coaches have already made up their "A-List" of recruits and narrowed it down to their top priority prospects. While it's important to have a productive senior year, understand that your junior year is much more important from a college coach's standpoint.

LESSON LEARNED: Play hard at all times, but remember that your junior year and the summer just before your senior year are the most important recruiting time period.

15. Coaches Need to Fill Lots of Roster Spots Each Year.

The numbers in the accompanying "Boxscore" are a rough estimate of how few college roster spots are available each year to players like you. They demonstrate how hard you will have to work and how pro-active you will need to be with your search if you are serious about wanting to play college ball.

According to our figures, your competition may include as many as 61,000 high school graduates and junior college players seeking to transfer to a four-year school. That doesn't even account for potential recruits in Puerto Rico, Australia, and Canada, also being pursued by college coaches.

As you can see in the chart, only 6,800 of these players, or 11 percent (1 out of every 9) will ever have the opportunity to play college baseball at any level. Some of them will receive athletic scholarships, but most will not. If you estimate how few players receive even partial baseball scholarships, the number is staggering.

LESSON LEARNED: Very few roster spots are available. You need to work hard both on and off the field to stand out from the crowd.

Over 60,000 Players Compete for the Chance to Play

	ASSUMPTIONS	H.S	J.C	TOTAL
TEAMS	Actual number of teams in the U.S.	15,720	377	16,097
PLAYERS	15 players/h.s. team and 25/JC team	235,800	9,425	245,225
GRADUATES	9 h.s. players/team and 15/ JC team	141,480	9,425	150,905
WANT TO PLAY	4 h.s. players/team and 8 JC players/team	56,592	4,713	61,305

Roster Spots Only Available for 1 Out of Every 9 Players Who Want to Play!

DIVISIONS #	SCHOOLS	ROSTER SIZE	FRESHMEN SPOTS*	% WHO PLAY
NCAA D-I	281	7,025	1,405	2%
NCAA D-II	214	5,350	1,070	2%
NCAA D-III	309	7,725	1,545	3%
NAIA	180	4,500	900	1%
NJCAA	377	9,425	1,885	3%
Total	1,361	34,025	6,805	11%

*Assumes each college class (freshmen, sophomore, junior, senior, fifth year senior) is 20% of the roster.

2
ENERGIZE YOUR SUPPORT GROUP

In This Chapter

- Do's and don'ts for parents who want to help
- Making your guidance counselor your advocate
- Your high school coach can be your secret weapon

You are definitely not alone in the process of solving the college-recruiting puzzle. There are many people ready and willing to help you if you just ask. Like a baseball general manager uses scouts and coaches to recommend players to draft and trade for, you need to develop your own cast of advocates, first to help you create a list of colleges best suited to you, and then to help you apply and gain admission.

This chapter helps you identify and energize the people who can improve your chances of reaching your college athletic and academic goals. It also includes some information specifically designed for your parents or guardians, the people who have the most at stake financially and emotionally in how your college selection process moves forward. So, even if they can't take the time to read this entire book, at least make sure they review this chapter with you.

PARENTS

It's a challenge to strike the right balance between offering guidance to your son and taking control of his entire college search process. If he is like most teenagers, you will need to constantly provide gentle reminders so he stays focused on the search.

In this chapter we discuss some of the ways to help him prepare for one of the biggest decisions and transitions of his young life. The objective: help him get accepted to a college where he will receive the best education possible and have the opportunity to play college baseball, in that order.

It's A Big Country, So Think National
The United States is blessed with many wonderful things, including the best, largest, and most diverse higher education system in the world. There are dozens of colleges that would be a good academic and athletic match for any high school baseball player, including your son.

The first commandment of developing a Target List of appropriate schools is to start with an open mind and a blank slate. "What's the right school for my son?" is a multiple-choice question with more than one right answer. Discourage him from fixating on a single "dream" school, unless he's an absolute lock to get in and is one of those unusual kids who knows exactly what he wants in life. Even then, we recommend you look at other institutions just in case he starts second guessing himself later on.

 If your plan for paying for your son's education is basically, "he will get a full-ride scholarship," you're probably in for a rude awakening. College athletic scholarships are hard to come by and most do not cover all of your child's expenses. It's great to win the lottery, but not too smart to plan on it happening.

It's Okay to Be Nervous, But Try Not To Grab The Wheel
Helping with the research and applying to colleges reminds you of the separation soon to come and the undeniable fact that your teenager is moving toward adulthood. This can make you nervous and emotional. You may feel tempted to take control of the evaluation and application process, particularly if he is not being as diligent and focused as you would like.

One simple word of advice: Don't! Your job is to support him in his efforts to make his own decision about college and his future. Managing this process on his own is a critical element in his mental and psychological preparation for leaving home. He can handle it and so can you!

As the process unfolds, remind him that because he applied to a variety of colleges, and also worked hard at his academics and baseball, he will be accepted to at least one of the schools on his Target List-one where he will make friends, have fun, be challenged, and get the education he deserves. When the decision letters arrive, re-emphasize your support, and if necessary, remind him of the fickle nature of the whole selection process.

Stay In the Background
Nothing is worse than a parent who steals the spotlight. Many parents, especially successful ones, are accustomed to manipulating the system to make it work for them. Resist the temptation. The admissions process is the time for your child to stand on his own. Parental attempts at influence peddling often do more harm than good.

Don't Live Vicariously
Many parents subconsciously relive their own hopes and dreams through their children. Some want their son to follow in their footsteps; others want them to achieve things that they themselves never could. Still other par-

ents see their child's college admission as proof they deserve an A+ in parenting. Having high hopes for your son is natural, but try to spare him the burden of unreasonable expectations. One of the greatest gifts you can give him is the freedom and the support to follow his own dreams, not yours.

Communicate

Encourage your son to think through the basic questions:
- Why do you want to go to college?
- What are your most important needs and goals?
- What size school would feel most comfortable?
- Do you want to stay close to home, driving distance or an airplane ride away?

Communicating with a teenager is not always easy, but look for the moments that present themselves, and they will. Being available to talk when he has a question or want to express an idea or feeling is extremely important. This is probably the first time he is dealing with a decision of this magnitude, so try to be patient and give him the time and space to find a way to communicate what his thoughts and fears are.

Set Financial Parameters

Although we have been stressing up to this point that the college selection process should be managed by your son, there is one part of this picture over which you have the responsibility and the obligation to assert your control: dollars and cents.

If you're in the market for a Chevrolet, it doesn't make sense to spend a lot of time at the Mercedes dealer ogling cars you can't afford. Likewise, if your resources can't support a tuition of $30,000 per year, have that conversation with your son before starting to develop a Target List of schools. This will be a necessary and healthy dose of real life for both of you.

You and your son will be terribly disappointed if you end up falling in love with a school and a program that is simply beyond your means, and you have to say "sorry, keep looking." Go on-line and find a list of all U.S. colleges sorted by tuition expense. Chapter 8 features a list of great web sites to help you with your research. No matter what your budget, your son is sure to find plenty of schools to choose from.

Be Realistic

Don't set him up for failure by encouraging him to apply only to schools that may be out of reach. Look honestly at his academic record and baseball ability, and then study the admissions profiles of the colleges on the Target List. If he is not Stanford material, don't swing by Palo Alto on your college tour. Make sure he applies to at least two colleges where he is over-qualified and can expect to be accepted. Then, even in the worst-case scenario, if he isn't accepted to his first choice schools, he still has a viable Plan B.

 Your perception of your child's athletic ability will not earn a scholarship. The college coach's opinion and other respected and objective appraisals are the only ones that matter.

Encourage Him to Stay On Schedule

Review the High School Checklist (see Chapter 8) with your son to make sure he is staying on track and doing the required work. Don't let him procrastinate and put it off until his senior year of high school. Players who do their research and prepare early have the most opportunities.

Support, Support, Support!

You can lighten the workload by providing guidebooks and web addresses, returning questionnaires, assisting with background research, and following the advice in this guide. Just make sure to stay in the background, in a supportive role. If you discover a potential gem of a school, pass along the web address and let him explore it for himself. Share your own college decision-making memories. Convey your understanding of how intimidating the process can seem and let him benefit from your experience.

Be a Cheerleader
Be generous with your praise for your son's accomplishments. Remind him that the acceptance or rejection to a particular school will not change his worth as an individual. The world is filled with highly accomplished people who didn't attend prestigious universities.

Encourage Your Child to Focus on Academics
The higher his grades and test scores, the more baseball opportunities he will have. Make academics a priority and do whatever is necessary to convey the importance of raising his marks. If his is not reaching his academic potential, find someone who can help him, whether it's a private tutor, a teacher, or one of his friends. Make sure that you make this assessment early on in his academic career so both of you will have time to increase his potential.

Senior year is too late to address this! Be aware that there are some student/athletes who figure that their senior year is a time to "take it easy" and enjoy their last year of high school. This is the time that some students' grades take a nosedive. Don't let this "senioritis" happen to your son! College admissions people frown on this and are aware of this phenomenon. It's not uncommon for an offer to be withdrawn in the event of a shoddy senior academic year.

"We want our recruits to be sound, solid people. They don't have to have the greatest grades in the world, but they should work hard for them. They need to understand that when students leave here, they will have to create a career for themselves." - Jeff Albies, Head Baseball Coach, William Patterson University, NCAA D-III

"Academic" Athletic Showcases
Some specialized showcases are now only inviting talented athletes with superior grades and/or SAT or ACT scores. These showcases are held for strong academic schools who are also interested in recruiting some top-flight athletes. Schools like Rice, Notre Dame, Stanford, and Northwestern University fit this category. Even though the Ivy League and Patriot League don't provide athletic scholarships, they often assist the athlete with academic scholarships and grants. Besides athletic ability, players invited to these specialized showcases may have to meet at least one of the following academic criteria: 3.3 grade point average, 1100 SAT score, or 24 ACT score.

Discuss Majors and Potential Careers
Talk about potential majors that may interest your son. Ask him what he would like to do for his career. He may not have an answer but it's something he should be thinking about. Encourage him to seek advice from successful family friends who work in his areas of interest. In many parts of the country there are opportunities for a high school student to "shadow" someone in the field they're interested in, i.e., spend a day on the job with that person. Also, there are often mentoring opportunities for students to be advised and guided by someone in the field they're interested in. Coaches are impressed by students who have clear career goals, or at least have put some thought into what they want to do after baseball. It's a sign of maturity many coaches appreciate and value.

Visit College Campuses
From the time your child enters high school, make an effort to visit as many different college campuses as you can. You can attend sporting events, concerts, or go on campus tours. Let him experience the colleges that you

or other family members attended. If your family takes vacations, visit schools in that area. Once your son reaches junior year of high school, limit your visits to schools that he is seriously considering. Schedule your trips so they have time to watch the baseball team practice or play a game. These unofficial visits will give them enormous insight and help decide what kind of school he wants to attend.

Get Periodic Updates
It is important to periodically phone or meet with your son's teachers, guidance counselor, and baseball coach. This will keep you informed of their progress and allow you to confirm that they are staying on course and meeting academic requirements.

Don't Write Your Child's Application Essay
Many colleges require essays as part of their application process. Advisors caution parents not to edit their son's essays, since admissions officers can distinguish easily between the writing of a 45-year-old and that of a 17-year-old. Instead, review the application folder for mistakes or omissions. Once it has been sent, do not call, write, or e-mail the admissions office. All communication should come from your son.

Stress a College Education, Not the Major League Draft
It's okay to support your son's dream of playing professional baseball straight out of high school, but we recommend you encourage him to apply to college anyway. That way, if your son doesn't get drafted ion June of his senior year of high school, he will still have productive options. If you wait until after the draft to start his college search, his options will often be limited to two-year schools. if your son has the potential to be drafted by a major league team, chances are he would also be highly attractive to college baseball coaches, so gaining admission to many schools should be easier.

"College gave me a few years to mature. I knew I wasn't ready to go to the pros straight out of high school. Going to college helped me grow up." - Joe Ausanio, former Major League Pitcher, New York Yankees

Step Aside
If your son gets rejected at a particular school, the worst thing you can do is call the school and tell them they overlooked something. Admission officers are more apt to listen to a direct appeal from your son than from a disappointed parent. Also, resist the temptation to call coaches and write letters on his behalf. Most college coaches would rather communicate with a player than a parent. It demonstrates that he is mature and responsible.

Split Up On College Visits
Many counselors advise parents to avoid the temptation of accompanying their son everywhere on campus. You may even want to skip the guided campus tour and let him experience it by himself. Most admissions officers won't allow parents into the interview but will entertain a few questions afterward. While you wander around campus, your son can sit in on classes, talk to professors and hang out with students.

Deal With Rejection
If the dreaded rejection letter arrives from your son's top-choice school, don't turn his disappointment into your own. With this response, he is apt to feel like he has failed you, too. Let him mourn his dream. Be around in case he wants to talk about it. Tell him that from your perspective, it doesn't matter where he goes to college. Say you are sorry and that you know he's disappointed. Leave it at that. Focus on the schools that accept him.

One Parent's Mistake
Alyssa Williams, New Haven, CT

In high school, my son Aaron was a three-year starter on the varsity team and was voted Team MVP his senior season. He wasn't the most dominant player in our region, but everyone knew who he was. I figured he would have college coaches offering scholarships to him. I couldn't have been more wrong! By the start of his junior season, I was expecting coaches to show up at his games to watch him play. Aaron expressed interest in a couple of college programs by sending introductory letters during the previous winter. He even got some responses back with questionnaires attached. After I met with his high school coach, I was confident the coach would use his connections to help get Aaron a baseball scholarship. His coach knew a lot of people at the collegiate level and assured me everything would work out.

As his senior season approached, a lot of Aaron's friends were getting accepted to schools. I told him to go out and put up the kind of stats he was capable of and everything would fall into place. Aaron finished his senior year as a member of the All-County team with a .448 BA, 12 HR, 47 RBI and 0 scholarship offers. They say mothers know best, but in this case, I didn't. I should have encouraged Aaron to take a more pro-active approach promoting himself to college coaches. Luckily, his grades were good enough to get accepted to a strong academic college. He was even the star centerfielder on his team… his fraternity's intramural squad.

GUIDANCE COUNSELOR

For better or worse, your guidance counselor is likely to play a crucial part in your college search and application process. He will write recommendations for you that, come April of your senior year, will help determine whether you receive fat envelopes full of enrollment materials or skinny ones with rejection letters.

A guidance counselor can monitor phone calls from admissions officers with questions about a low grade on your transcript or a discipline problem. And if you wind up getting rejected everywhere you applied, a sympathetic counselor might even plead your case to admissions officials at schools that still have open slots. These are professionals you definitely want in your corner, so don't be shy about making the first move. It's also advantageous to include someone whose primary perspective is academic.

Learn Your Way Around The Office
While your guidance counselor is getting to know you, get to know your counselor's resources. Ask for a tour of the guidance office and have the counselor recommend college guidebooks, videotapes, and web sites. Find out whether your high school hosts workshops on college admissions. If it does, you should attend every session possible.

Use Your Counselor's Connections
Your best college resource may be your counselor's connections. If your counselor visits a lot of campuses and invites many admissions officers to your school, he's probably plugged into the college admissions scene. Admissions officers who know and trust him may call for the inside scoop on you. And he will know which schools are most likely to accept you, which ones should be considered as "safeties" and which ones are long shots. We're stating the obvious here, but, take advantage of this professional's knowledge!

Provide Good (and Bad) Information
If your counselor is too swamped for frequent personal chats with you, drop off a resume that lists your recent accomplishments. Create a portfolio of your best papers and creative projects, and don't be shy about disclosing any family situations that may affect your academic performance. For instance, if one of your parents gets seriously ill and your grades slip as a result, tell your counselor so he can explain the situation in his recommendation. Once you establish a personal rapport with your counselor, e-mail may be a more acceptable way to stay in touch on routine matters.

Regular Meetings
Your counselor should meet with you and your parents for a conference at least once in your junior year and again early in your senior year. Topics can include your academic strengths and weaknesses, baseball, test scores, whether you should take a prep class, and suggestions for colleges to consider. He can also confirm if you are in compliance with NCAA eligibility requirements, explore potential career opportunities, identify colleges that specialize in your area of interest, and discuss the pros and cons of each school on your Target List.

Although most counselors are conscientious and knowledgeable, occasionally they may make an honest mistake, which could cost you a scholarship. Here's a real-life example of a high school player who took Spanish I in junior high (8th grade) and Spanish II and III as a freshman and sophomore in high school.

His guidance counselor said that colleges would consider that as having three years of a language. As it turned out, that was true of the state university where he lived, but wasn't for lots of out-of-state colleges, who only counted it as two years. The young man failed to qualify at the school he wanted to play at, which happened to be an out-of-state school with different requirements.

The point is-make sure you check out and know the academic requirements of the school(s) you'd like to play for and attend. A good place to start is to check the NCAA Eligibility site, as well as the school's admissions office.

Overcoming Failure
by Tom Hanson, Ph.D.

"Baseball is a game of failure." That's a line you hear often, and in many ways, it's true. There aren't many places in life you can "fail" 70% of the time and be considered great! Here are two of the best ideas I've learned from some of the best players in the history of the game for overcoming the inevitable adversity baseball throws at you:

Redefine "failure." Your personal statistics and your team's record are outside of your control. You can influence them, but not control them. Focus your energies on things you can control: your preparation, your focus, your attitude, and your commitment. If you define success as doing a great job with the things you can control, and failure as focusing on things you can't control, you'll give yourself the best chance of competing at a top level AND be a lot happier!

Focus on this moment. There's nothing you can do about the past, and nothing you can do now about the future. NOW is where the action is: this pitch! The great athletes keep it simple, and one way to do that is to keep your focus consistent. If you've had a bad day, go ahead and feel bad for awhile, that's okay. But remember, your poor performance is in the PAST. Before you go to bed that night, shift your focus to what you can control NOW: getting yourself into the best possible mindset for tomorrow's game or practice.

These ideas are simple, but not easy. Partner up with a buddy, coach, or parent to help you stay focused.

Tom Hanson, Ph.D., is a mental toughness coach who helps athletes; coaches and parents produce breakthrough results. Last year he worked full-time for theN ew York Yankees, and previously consulted with the Texas Rangers, Anaheim Angels and Minnesota Twins.

Help Developing a Plan and Timetable
Many counselors believe their job is not to tell students where to apply, but to advise them how to go about the process. Doing the legwork for students, counselors say, won't teach them the survival skills they need for college. A good counselor will direct you toward books and online resources. We will direct you to Chapter 4 where we tell you how to identify appropriate colleges for you and develop what we call your Target List.

Use History to Help You
Generally, high schools keep lists of where previous students have and haven't been accepted. Schools with more sophisticated programs also maintain a database on the records of students who were accepted and rejected at various colleges. Counselors should analyze the data to track athletic admissions trends and use them to guide applicants. Organized feedback from high school graduates about what they like and dislike about their colleges, and about how prepared they felt academically, is also useful information for you.

Be Vigilant
If you are put on a waiting list at your first-choice college, your counselor can call the college to promote you

and let the admissions department know you really want to go there. If the outlook is dim, your counselor can provide suggestions about alternatives. If a qualified student strikes out everywhere (a high school's worst nightmare), a dedicated counselor will call around to find out which colleges have space available.

Find a Counselor Who Will Help
While it may be tempting to avoid your counselor, that's almost always a mistake. If your counselor resists all advances or simply doesn't know enough about colleges to be helpful, make an appointment with another counselor at your school. If asked, tell your assigned counselor that you are doing it as a way to gather additional information.

You can also consider going outside the school for college advice. But be warned that your high school counselor can't be avoided entirely. He still writes your recommendation, and colleges will still call him, not the independent advisor, if a school wants to know more about you. Never fear, though. College admissions committees know that, for a variety of reasons, not everyone receives adequate counseling - or a fair recommendation.

Counselors-For-Hire
You could hire an educational consultant to help you develop a list of schools and prepare applications. Their services usually cost from $700 to several thousand dollars (ouch!). Princeton Review and Kaplan Test Prep and Admissions also offer one-on-one counseling. Less personalized counseling is also available in seminars or online packages. If you are truly needy, you can turn to groups such as Bottom Line, which counsels students for free. Many pricey consultants also offer free counseling; so don't be afraid to ask.

Red Flags
Ask prospective counselors for professional references and call them. A few things to avoid: inexperienced consultants who claim their Ivy League degrees give them special insight into the admission process; independent counselors who have cantankerous relationships with guidance offices (you can't afford to alienate your high school counselor!); and consultants who promise entrance into prestigious schools before viewing your academic record. It sounds too good to be true because it is.

A Guidance Counselor's Plea
Richard Douds, High School Guidance Counselor, Raleigh, NC

I get paid to give advice. I only wish more students would make me earn my money. A lot of students come to me for academic advice, but I'm equally qualified to help them advance athletically. My high school guidance counselor played baseball for Wake Forest University and knew what the recruiting process was all about. He helped me get a baseball scholarship using his connections, and I would love to do the same for my kids. Unfortunately, they don't come to me for help.

Aside from office resources, I have a number of connections to Division III schools on the east coast. Some of the coaches my kids have contacted me for recommendations. It's tough for me to promote someone if they haven't taken the time to come see me first. Once I get to know him on a personal level, it's easier to give college coaches the information they want. I would love to help students develop a plan to achieve their goals. Many of my colleagues don't know a lot about the recruiting process and wouldn't know what to say to a student looking to play at the collegiate level. I tell them to have their students come talk to me if they want advice. It's really no burden. I have no problem calling college coaches to promote one of our athletes, but he needs to make the effort to come see me first.

HIGH SCHOOL COACH

Take Responsibility For Your College Search.
Do not depend on your high school coach to research potential schools, phone coaches on your behalf, or eventually land you a college scholarship. If your high school coach is supportive and wants to help you, consider yourself fortunate and be sure to thank him.

Don't worry, however, if your high school coach is not as involved as you would like and only devotes time to team practices and games. Even though you would like to believe your coach is responsible for helping you with your college search, it is not officially part of his job responsibilities. Remember, you have many teammates who would like the same kind of personal interest from him. So, if your coach wants to help you, gratefully accept his assistance. If he doesn't make the offer, or respond to your request, take full responsibility for your future.

Ask Your High School Coach to Initiate Dialogue With Your Target Coaches
After you mail your Letter of Interest and Athlete Profile to your Target List (see Chapter 5), ask your high school coach if he would be willing to do some or all of the following:
- Write an evaluation of you and send it to your target schools.
- Phone each coach on your Target List to confirm the school's interest in you and give a verbal recommendation.
- Clarify the college's decision-making process.
- Stimulate interest if the coach is not recruiting you.
- Help you with your highlight video

Use Other Sources for Help
Find someone who will assist you if your high school coach cannot. This person must be someone who has credibility and is familiar with your skills:
- Opposing high school coach
- College coach
- Pro Scout
- Former pro player who gives you lessons
- Summer league coach
- Baseball alumnus in your sport of one of your target schools

A High School Coach's Conflict
Coach Mike Rivera, Baltimore MD

My students assume my day starts at 7:20 AM. In reality, my day starts well before that. My 30-minute commute north from Annapolis starts around 6:30 AM and I'm awake an hour before that. I teach math five out of eight periods and also hold advising and office hours. When I'm not in the classroom, I'm grading tests, tutoring students, and devising lesson plans. A lot of my students end their day with the last bell around 1:45 PM. At this point, I've been out of my house for nearly eight hours and my day is only beginning.

At the end of eighth period, I replace lesson plans with game plans. Aside from my duties in the classroom, I'm also the head coach in two different sports. I hold daily practices from 2:30-5:00 PM, and on game days, we're usually done around 8:00 PM. Fifteen-hour days are tough, especially with a 1/2 hour commute tacked on each way.

A lot of my players ask me to help them get scholarships, and I do the best I can to assist them, but there isn't enough time in the day. I try to write evaluations for all my players and call college coaches on their behalf, but I can't help everyone. I know how stressful the recruiting and college selection process can be on my players and their parents, which puts me in an awkward situation.

I would love to help all of my players get scholarships, but it's more important for me to see my students pass math. First and foremost, I'm a teacher. When I was a kid, I used to eat, sleep, and breathe sports. Now, I'm lucky if I have time to simply eat and sleep.

BOTTOM OF THE NINTH

Part of the recruiting process is taking stock of your assets for a college's team and its admissions department. And part of getting recruited is taking stock of the assets you have to draw on during the process itself.

Sit down, separately, with your parents, coach, and counselor. Tell them about your goals and dreams for college. Ask them for help in the process, and come to an agreement about how much help they will provide, and what type(s) of help it will be. Then, make a list of all your resources and determine how you will use them to help you get recruited.

3
HOW TO IMPROVE YOUR PROFILE

In This Chapter

- Improving your approach to the game
- Enhancing the mental aspects of your game
- Developing your leadership abilities
- Improving your physical skills
- Increasing your grades and test scores
- Staying focused in the classroom

No matter how many compliments you've received about your play, your grades, or your personality, there are always ways you can improve.

This chapter focuses on ways to improve your profile (and no, we don't mean the side view of your face), so that you are more "recruitable" by college coaches.

BASEBALL SUGGESTIONS

At the risk of stating the obvious, your baseball ability is the most important factor in determining whether you will suit up in a college uniform. Never assume that you are finished learning as a player or that you know everything about the game. You must constantly absorb information and strive to improve your ability. This may mean shaving half a second off your 60-yard dash time, learning to hit with more power, or adding 5 mph to your fastball.

Even Major Leaguers spend hundreds of hours in the off-season working on the physical and mental aspects of their game, so you know there's no such thing as too much practice.

Understand what's in your control to improve. Some physical characteristics like your height and body structure may not change, but there are areas within your control that you can improve. These areas include:
- Running speed
- Arm strength, agility
- Batting power
- Fielding mechanics
- Leadership ability
- Attitude

You'll have to work extremely hard and demonstrate unyielding motivation in order to separate yourself from the thousands of other players competing with you for a spot on a college roster.

If you know you are weak in a particular aspect of your event do something about it...now! Don't accept the fact that you're not as fast on the bases or as powerful a hitter as you'd like to be. How many people told Mugsy Bogues that a 5-foot-3 point guard could never play college basketball, let alone star in the NBA? Did you know that Michael Jordan was cut from his high school basketball team? Fortunately, these two players refused to give up. Do you have that same tenacity?

Seek Constructive Criticism
In order to improve, first identify which areas of your game needs work. It's always nice to hear praise from your parents and receive backslaps from your teammates, but a little constructive criticism from the experts is even better. Instead of relying on your parents' opinion of your skills, consult an experienced high school coach, college coach, or pro scout who has seen you compete. He or she can tell you the exact areas to improve and recommend specific drills to help you.

Seek as many opinions as you can. For example, ask your coach to be completely honest and forthcoming about your strengths and weaknesses. You may not agree with his evaluation, but you can use it as a starting point for your development. It is also important to respect his opinion and let him know that you are going to consider his advice. In addition to learning where your game could use some improving, make sure you set aside the time for drills to help turn your weaknesses into strengths.

If you have mechanical flaws in your batting, fielding, pitching, or base running, you must fix them immediately to avoid making them a permanent part of your technique. Videotaping yourself in a practice setting is an excellent way for you to recognize exactly what you are doing wrong and it's a great way to solicit feedback from others who haven't seen you play much or at all. Then, work tirelessly in practice and at home to create new muscle memory based on hitting, fielding and throwing the correct way. If you don't drill your muscles and your mind in practice, you can be sure those bad habits will return under the pressure of game time situations.

Take Your Game To The Coaches

Exposure is key to the recruiting process. The more coaches who see you play, the better chance you have to generate interest. Don't wait for coaches to come to you. Be pro-active and take your game to them.

Your goal should be to generate as much national interest as you can, so you will have a wide array of options when it comes time to sign a National Letter of Intent. If you live in New York and want to compete in North Carolina, you better make sure southern coaches see you compete in person. It is unusual for a coach to offer a scholarship to a player no one on his staff has seen compete. It's too much of a risk.

That's why you need to find out how you can compete in front of the coaches on your Target List. Call each school and ask the coach what events his recruiters are attending. Also, ask them to put you on their mailing list to be notified when winter and summer camps are conducted (as well as any special camps), and any other pertinent information. Just make sure the coaches on your Target List see you in action.

How Many of These Leadership Qualities Do You Possess?

- Have a strong desire to win and always do your best.
- Seek tough competition.
- Welcome a difficult task.
- Set high, but achievable goals.
- Be willing to admit mistakes and accept constructive criticism.
- Practice on your own - go beyond what your coach asks of you.
- Enjoy the responsibility that accompanies leadership.
- Be willing to work harder than anyone else, especially when the coach is not watching.
- Possess confidence in your ability.
- Focus and concentrate on the task at hand.
- Learn from your mistakes and try not to repeat them.
- Maintain composure - never throw your bat or helmet in anger.
- Don't get easily discouraged or frustrated by errors, mistakes, or poor officiating.
- Understand the importance of continuous coaching.
- Respect your parents, coaches, umpires, teammates, and opponents.
- Put the team's needs before your personal needs.
- Get along with your teammates - offer support when they have a problem.
- Understand that championships are won in the pre-season.
- Watch your language and avoid profanity.
- Encourage your teammates and do not belittle your opponents.
- Maintain a positive appearance and good body language.

WHAT MOTIVATES A WINNER...
Coach Rob Kelso, University of Houston

- A winner displays characteristics that set him apart from all others.
- A winner always wants to be the best that he can be.
- A winner is never satisfied with his performance. He is committed to preparing and open to change, and always wants to succeed, whether it's a high GPA or a better athletic performance.
- A winner learns from his failures and he never makes excuses.
- A winner always looks for ways to improve his performance and to add value to the team.
- A winner always expects to be victorious.
- A winner is not afraid of risk.

Arm Strength & Running Times to Strive For

by Jim Grief, Cincinnati Reds pro scout

Here are some guidelines that you should strive to reach by your junior year of high school. Keep in mind that these numbers are estimates and there are exceptions to every rule.

Arm Strength
Catchers:
Pop to pop time (from the moment the ball hits the catchers glove until the moment the ball hits the second baseman's glove) should be 2.1 seconds or less. The major league average is 1.9 seconds, yet Ivan Rodriguez does it in 1.7 seconds!

Pitchers:
Left-handers should throw at least 77 mph. Right-handers should throw at least 81 mph. All pitchers should have good movement and excellent control.

Outfielders:
Throw at least 81 mph from deep right field to the infield.

Shortstop & Third Basemen:
Throw at least 80 mph from deep SS to 1B.

Second Basemen:
Throw at least 76 mph from deep SS to 1B.

Running Times
Home to First
Righty Batter:
- 4.6 seconds - average high school player
- 4.4 seconds - average college player
- 4.2 seconds or below will impress a college coach or pro scout

Lefty Batter:
- 4.5 seconds - average high school player
- 4.3 seconds - average college player
- 4.1 seconds or below will impress a college coach or pro scout

60-Yard Dash
High School:
- 7.6 seconds - average player
- 7.2 seconds or below will impress a college coach or pro scout

Pro Player:
- 7.0 seconds - average player
- 7.2 seconds - average 3B/1B/C/power-hitting OF
- 6.8 seconds - average SS/2B/speed OF
- 6.2 seconds - Alfonso Soriano

Stay In Shape
It is extremely important to stay in shape year-round. Take your cue from the pros who work hard in the off-season to stay fit. Do not become inactive at any time and don't stay away from the game for more than a few weeks at a time. Even if you're busy with fall or winter sports, find some time every week to have a catch, visit a batting cage, and shag some fly balls or field grounders. Staying in top physical form demonstrates to college coaches that you are serious about your commitment to baseball and your future. Also, it's good for your health and will improve your academic effectiveness.

Become A Leader
Coaches admire athletes who demonstrate a winning attitude, mental toughness, a passion for the game, and composure under pressure. These traits will not only make you a better player, but they will help you elevate the games of your teammates as well. So, be a leader, not a follower. If you're not one of those "verbal types," lead by example with your work ethic in practice and your desire to improve. If you are one of those guys who likes to talk to your teammates, keep it positive and enthusiastic. Strive to be someone who is described by his coach and teammates as a "student of the game," a "great team player," and a "winner."

How do you handle failure? Do you get overly upset, blame coaches, umpires, teammates, your parents? If you fail, yet contine to hustle, that is just what college coaches want. Remeber the only things you can control when playing sports are your attitude, concentration, and effort. Control the controllable's.

"One of the qualities we look for in our players is if they hustle every play, another is how they react to failure. We want positive players who keep their composure after making a mistake." - Jim Brady, Head Baseball Coach, University of Missouri-St. Louis, NCAA D-II

Attend Prospect Camps at Your Top Target Schools
Most college baseball coaches run their own instructional summer camp for high school athletes. These camps are usually 1-2 weeks long and packed with intense instruction, chalk talks, and game situations. Once you've narrowed down your college choices, think seriously about attending prospect camps run by the coaches at your top schools. It is an ideal opportunity to gain exposure with their recruiting staff, get a feel for what these coaches are looking for, and visit the campus. From the coaches standpoint, they are getting to know you as a person and a player, evaluating not only your talent but whether you would be a good fit in their system.

Improve Your Arm Strength
College coaches recruit players who have strong arms, regardless of what position they play. From a college coach's perspective, a good high school player can be taught to play any position, as long as he has the requisite arm strength. In other words, there aren't many spots on the field for weak arms. Even a second baseman needs to be able to throw the ball to first on a double play with velocity and accuracy. To see how you measure up, check out the minimum radar gun requirements that some coaches use on page 35. Consult your high school coach to see how you can safely and gradually build your arm strength.

Increase Your Foot Speed
One of the best ways to impress a college coach is with your speed. Contrary to what some people say, speed can be taught. It's possible for you to become a faster base runner and cover more ground on defense, if you follow a good training program. "Speed kills" is a popular way to describe the advantage to a baseball team that overwhelms opponents by being quicker and faster. Fast base runners force errors by hurried fielders, pitchers are distracted by hitters who can get out of the box quickly or steal abase, and opposing hitters start pressing when defensive speed shrinks the open field. So get to work on getting out of the batter's box faster, getting a better jump on the ball in the field, and moving from base to base in less time. There is no substitute for just getting out there every day and working to overcome your weaknesses.

Play For a Competitive Summer Team

Here are some of the top sumemr league programs for you to consider:

United States Specialty Sports Association
P.O Box 1998 - 3935 S. Crater Rd.
Petersburg, VA 23805
Web: www.usssa.com
Phone: 804-732-4099

American Legion Baseball
P.O. Box 1055
Indianapolis, IN 46206
Web: www.legion.org
Phone: 317-630-1434

Amateur Athletic Union
P.O. Box 10000
Lake Buena Vista, Fl 32803
Web: www.aausports.org
Phone: 407-934-7200

Babe Ruth Baseball
1770 Brunswick Pike, P.O. Box 5000
Trenton, NJ 08638
Web: www.baberuthleague.org
Phone: 609-695-1434

Pony Baseball
P.O. Box 225
Washington, PA 15301
Web: www.pony.org
Phone: 724-225-1060

American Amateur Baseball Congress
118-119 Redfield Plaza, P.O. Box 467
Marshall, MI 49068
Web: www.voyager.net/aabc/
Phone: 616-781-2002

National Amateur Baseball Federation
P.O. Box 705
Bowie, MD 20715
Web: www.nabf.com
Phone: 301-262-5005

5 Keys for Optimal Performance
by Matt Tauber, President & Owner, TruFit Sport & Athletic Training, P.C.

In order to excel in any sport, it is important that you maintain a year-round strength and conditioning regimen. Consult a certified trainer to help you develop a custom program that fits your needs. Make sure it includes the following five components:

1. Sport-specific speed, agility, and quickness drills.
2. Baseball-specific movements to develop muscular power, strength and endurance. Train movements, not individual muscles.
3. Adequate rest and recovery.
4. Proper nutrition
5. Flexibility training.

Matt Tauber is a certified athletic trainer who ownsN ew York-based TruFit Sport & Athletic Training, P.C. He can be reached at trainer33@aol.com or 914-414-6241

A Behind-the-Scenes Look at What Criteria a College Coach Uses When Evaluating Your Ability

By Richard Todd, President, Webball.com

Evaluating Your Body Control
You will need to show ability with your first-step quickness, fielding balls hit to both the glove side and throwing side, timing jumps, and charging the ball to come up throwing. This requires good anticipation, quick feet, and hands that are both soft and quick to adjust to bad hops and absorb sharply hit line drives.

Evaluating Your Arm Strength During Infield/Outfield Practice
Outfielders: Coaches want to see a strong overhand throw, a straight-line trajectory, good carry, and good life on the turf when the ball finally hits the ground. The right fielder needs the strongest arm.

Infielders: Coaches want to see a straight-line trajectory, a strong hissing noise when the ball is in the air, and a sharp smack in the receiving player's glove. A strong arm is necessary for shortstop and third basemen. Coaches will pay the most attention to throws made from the outfield grass at deep shrot. Shortstops often make throws of up to 150 feet flat-footed on the edge of the outfield grass. Third baseman need to make strong throws of up to 120 feet from along the foul line.

Evaluating Your Hitting
Hitting is among the most difficult tools to scout because the recruiters must predict how you will do at the college level while watching you hit against high school pitching. Coaches will focus on you mechanics and ability to anticipate and react, not your statistics:

1. **Swing a Quick Bat** You bat speed - the ability to whip the bat quickly and smoothly through the strike zone - is important for handling breaking pitches and hitting for power. If you have a quick bat, you can wait on pitches longer, and have a better chance of hitting the ball harder.

2. **Hit the Ball Hard and with Power** Coaches will pay close attention to your bat speed and your hand position when you stride. Dropping or raising your hands during the pitch delivery decreases your chance of hitting the ball hard. Your hands should go back, and the less movement, the better.

3. **Turn on a Fastball** You should be able to pull a hard fastball thrown on the inside part of the plate.

4. **Hit Breaking Pitches** You must be able to hit breaking pitches or you will not survive at the college level. Once word gets out about your inability to hit a breaking pitch, you will see nothing else from a pitcher.

5. **Make Adjustments** When a pitcher changes his delivery, location or speed, poor hitters will lunge, not keep their hands back, develop a hitch or have a pronounced uppercut. The more patient a hitter you are, the more dangerous you become.

6. **Possess Knowledge of the Strike Zone** This means reading the pitch, having a consistent stance at the plate, and the understainding the umpire's strike zone.

7. **Hit to All Fields** A good hitter will go with the pitch and drive it hard to all fields. This ability relies on having quick hips and hands, good arm extension, and the proper follow-through motion.

Web Ball, which was founded by Richard Todd, is an on-line baseball skills clinic and web store filled with instructional diagrams and tips for players and coaches. For more information, go to www.webball.com.

10 Tips to Help You Run a Faster 60-Yard Dash

Speed never has an off day and it wins ball games! That's why college coaches like to fill their rosters with players who can run fast. Here are a few simple things you can do at your next showcase or prospect camp to lower your running time substantially.

1. **Warm-up Properly** Stretch your hamstrings, quads, and groin, and even take a practice run at 75% effort. If you warm-up properly your muscles will be loose and less likely to be injured.

2. **Get a Good Jump** Anticipate the start and stay low during the first few strides until you can work your way up to your upright running position.

3. **Run in a Straight Line** The shortest distances between two points is a straight line so stay close to the chalk mark.

4. **Run on the Balls of Your Feet** The less contact your feet make with the ground the better. Jumping rope is an excellent exercise to develop this habit. Also, practice high leg kicks (knees to chest) to improve your leg explosion.

5. **Keep Your Arms Moving in a Fluid and Straight Motion** Your fingers and palm should grace your cheek on your upstroke and your hip or butt on your downstroke (Remember "cheek to cheek"). Do not flail your arms wildly.

6. **Keep Your Face, Neck, and Shoulder Muscles Relaxed** Tensing your muscles will only slow you down. Also try to keep your mouth open while you run.

7. **Speed Up at the Finish Line** Pretend you're being timed for an extra 10 yards and run at full speed past the finish line. Avoid the temptation to slow down as you cross the tape.

8. **Take Off Your Hat** This will prevent the impulse to grab it if your hat starts to fall off while you're running.

9. **Match Yourself Against the Fastest Player** If two players in the group run at the same time, the competition will encourage you to pick it up a notch.

10. **Run Multiple Times** If your first run produces a low time, see if running again is allowed in an effort to lower your time.

Take Practice Seriously

You're in for a big surprise if you think a college coach only wants to watch you in a game situation. Often, a coach is more interested in seeing you practice or go through a pre-game warm-up than an actual game. Why? Because it can be a lot easier to evaluate your ability while you take 50 swings in the cage and field 20 grounders before the game then during a game in which you may not get a chance to make a defensive play and you may walk all four times at bat.

So, treat your pre-game routing like a game-time audition. Execute sound fundamentals whether you are taking ground balls, shagging flies or swinging the bat in BP. Don't act like a hit dog, stand around watching what other players are doing, or demonstrate a lackadaisical attitude toward the game. To put it simply, if you want to get noticed, work and play harder than anyone else around you does. Be the first player on the field and the last one to leave. You never know who is watching you. Since coaches rarely wear their school uniform or announce that they are in the stands, assume that someone important is watching you every time you step on the field.

Coaches know that the best indicator of how you will perform in a game is how you practice. It also tells a coach a lot about your approach to the game and whether you really understand what it takes to succeed at the next level. To an experienced eye, it's fairly easy to separate the pretenders from the contenders, even in practice.

Watch Instructional Videos

If you have trouble hitting a curve ball, would like to add a change-up to your pitching repertoire, want to steal more bases, or want to improve your mental toughness, there's a video you can buy to help you achieve your objective. While a video is no substitute for actual practice, it allows you to form a mental picture of what you want to achieve and how to go about it. Plus, you can watch a video over and over. There are hundreds of videos produced by experts on every physical and mental aspect of the game. Be sure to check out many websites, such as www.MyCoachOnline.com, which are home to such instructional videos. Whether they dramatically improve your overall game, or just help in one aspect, videos are well worth the investment.

Play With the Best Competition

If you're not a star player being actively scouted by college coaches, here's a sure fire way to get yourself in front of these talent evaluators: compete with or against blue-chip players that are being scouted! There are several reasons why you should do this:
- Playing with athletes better than you is an excellent way to improve your game.
- You will benefit from the enormous exposure that the blue-chip players receive.

Who cares if the coaches showed up to scout someone else? If you impress them, you can steal the limelight and create opportunities for yourself that might not have existed before. Don't be afraid to challenge yourself by stepping up the level of your competition.

Hire a Private Instructor

If you can afford it, go for it. A private baseball coach can really help you improve your skills. The effect of intensive one-on-one training and work outs can be dramatic. If you are fortunate enough to have the resources to work with a private instructor, it could be one of the best investments you make. As an alternative, see if you can find your way to a nearby college player who would consider instructing you for a reduced fee. Whether it's a college athlete or professional instructor you are considering, check his references and credentials before you hire him to make sure he understands the game and is a good teacher. If he graduated from one of your target schools or knows someone who did, even better!

ACADEMIC SUGGESTIONS

Before a college coach decides if he is going to recruit you, he looks at your GPA, core courses, and SAT/ACT scores to make sure you meet his school's admission standards. If you are way below the minimum requirements, he will not waste his time recruiting you, regardless of how much you could help his baseball team. Poor grades assure you of only one thing when it comes to college admissions and baseball: fewer choices.

If you're the best player in the league, can pitch 95 mph fastballs, or hit 450-foot home runs, junior college will be your only option if you are not strong enough academically to be admitted to a four-year school. Even an All-State caliber player with a poor track record in the classroom will give a scholarship-equipped coach pause.

Coaches know that athletes who don't perform in class are more likely to become academically ineligible or flunk out at the college level. And that may be more risk than a coach is willing to take. If a coach has only one scholarship left and he must choose between two athletes of equal talent, he will always select the better student.

Improve Your Grades and More Schools Will Be Able To Recruit You

Say, for example, you have a 2.6 GPA and 1300 SAT score. While those marks are average, you've automatically taken yourself off the recruiting lists of probably 500 strong academic schools! Imagine how many more opportunities you will have if you meet the admission requirements of all 1,343 schools with baseball programs in the country, or at least a higher percentage of them?

"Academically, we're not going to recruit any players who are question marks. Now I'm not saying he has to be a 3.5 student with 1650 SAT score, but I'm talking about a solid student. He has to understand the priority of college. He's here to get an education first." - Mike Martin, Head Baseball Coach, Florida State University, NCAA D-I

Consider that a school you're interested in may have very different requirements, peculiar to that school, and you need to be aware of those if they exist. For instance, in California, getting into the top state-sponsored universities (University of California system) requires very good grades as well as very specific requirements for high school classes. A biology class you took in your high school in Nebraska may not have the content they require.

Other schools in other states often have similar "extra" requirements. Check out each school you're interested in to make sure the classes you take will qualify. There has been more than one instance of a student/athlete who has graduated from high school with good grades and met all the Clearinghouse requirements... and still was unable to meet the college entrance requirements of a particular school.

While this isn't the norm, it still happens often enough that you need to be prepared, which means you should try to identify as early as possible the school(s) you're interested in and make sure they don't have "above and beyond" requirements you still have time to do something about!

Set high goals for yourself in each class you take. Do not settle for mediocrity. Be disciplined with your homework and strive to reach your full potential. If you're receiving B's right now, go for A's. Ask your teacher for extra help, hire a tutor, form a study group with your friends, or take a preparatory SAT/ACT course. Take Advanced Placement (AP) classes if you can qualify for them.

Do whatever it takes to improve your academic standing and do not believe for one second that grades are unimportant. Nothing impresses a college coach more than athletes who work just as hard in the classroom as they do on the playing field.

Manage Your Time Effectively

Since your daily schedule is already filled with classes, sports, and extracurricular activities, it's important you set aside a block of time each night for homework and your college search. Make it a priority and be disciplined. You will reap the rewards for many years to come.

Develop Other Interests And Get Involved In Extracurricular Activities

College admission officers look favorably on students who have multiple interests and are involved in a wide range of activities. Find an organization at your school (i.e. school newspaper, Safe Rides, Drama Club, Band, Foreign Language Club, etc.) that interests you and get involved. Also, you may want to consider volunteering a few hours each month at a local charity or non-profit organization.

Don't worry about trying to become a "Renaissance Man or Woman" at age 17. Not many high school seniors are the perfect, well-rounded student. Just show a passion for one or two of your strongest interests. Do not simply build a resume that lists every club in your school. What impresses admission officers is proof that an activity is a theme in your life...think quality, not quantity.

Recently, a counselor urged one student, a TV-sports addict, to get off the couch and get involved. The student started writing a sports column for the high school paper, coaching basketball in a poor neighborhood, and interning at an all-sports television channel. The counselor is betting that he'll have several admissions offers to choose from next year.

Work To Increase Your GPA

If you did not perform well in your freshman year of high school, you may be given the benefit of the doubt if your grades go up in your sophomore, junior, and senior years. Your goal should be to graduate ranked as high as possible in your class. And, by all means, avoid "senioritis." Don't think that you can coast as soon as your applications are finished. Colleges will notice if you drop an AP course, take an easy schedule, or let your GPA slide in your senior year. Some schools will even pull admission offers from a student who performs poorly in his senior year.

Hire A Tutor or Enroll In A SAT/ACT Preparation Course

Ask your guidance counselor for suggestions to raise your college entrance exam scores. Kaplan and Princeton Review offer outstanding courses you may want to consider. Taking a prep course will boost your confidence tremendously. Some students hire private tutors or purchase computer study programs.

If you have to, take these exams several times until you are satisfied with your scores. Regardless of which exams you take, don't assume a higher-than-average score will guarantee acceptance to your dream school. Test scores are not weighted as heavily as most people think they are, although very poor scores can be difficult to overcome. It's just another part of the package.

Take Advanced Placement or College-Level Courses

College admission officers will view you as a motivated student if your high school transcript features some honors and AP courses. Your GPA may slide a little, but it's worth it to take advanced classes in areas where you are strong.

For example, if you've always received good grades in math, take AP calculus and AP statistics. If writing and reading are your strong points, take AP English. Remember, your transcript is the most important piece of your application. Many admission officers would rather see you challenge yourself than get straight A's in easy courses. Many colleges "weight" AP classes by scoring them half a grade higher than "regular" courses for the student's GPA.

Spend Your Summers Productively
Admissions deans don't look kindly on summers spent relaxing at the beach or on the couch, but otherwise they're surprisingly open-minded. If you need money, take that fast-food restaurant job, and then try to make the experience as meaningful as you can. You might sign up for a community college course or summer enrichment program, for example, or do volunteer work.

Take Both Entrance Exams
Virtually all colleges accept both the SAT and ACT, so you may want to take them both and just feature the better score on your application. To determine which you'll find easier, take a practice version of each and compare your scores using a concordance table (www.collegeboard.com has one available online).

Standardized Test Information

PSAT/NMSQT (as of Fall 2004) - Math, Verbal, Critical Reading, Writing Skills
Length & Type - 2 hours and 10 minutes - multiple choice
Purpose - The PSAT helps you prepare for the SAT and determine your eligibility for the National Merit Scholarship
Registration & Fees - www.collegeboard.com
(609) 771-7070
Register with your college Advisor

NEW SAT I Reasoning Test (as of Spring 2005) - Math, Critical Reading & Writing (essay)
Length & Type - 3 hours and 45 minutes - multiple choice and essay
Purpose - The most common exam required by U.S. colleges and universities
Registration & Fees - www.collegeboard.com
(609) 771-7600

New ACT (as of February 2005) - English, Math, Reading, Science & Writing (optional)
Length & Type - 2 hours and 55 minutes - multiple choice and essay
Purpose - Common Exam required by U.S. colleges and universities
Registration & Fees - www.act.org
(800) 525-6926

SAT II Subject Tests - Math, languages, Literature, Social Studies, Sciences
Length & Type - 1 hour - majority being multiple choice
Purpose - Some colleges require subject tests for admissions
Registration & Fees - www.collegeboard.com
(609) 771-7600

AP Exams (Advanced Placement) - Math, languages, Literature, Social Studies, Sciences
Length & Type - 3 hours - multiple choice and free response
Purpose - Some colleges award course credit to students who do well in these exams
Registration & Fees - www.collegeboard.com
(888) CALL-4-AP

TOEFL (Test of English as a Foreign language) - Listening, Reading, Writing.
As of September 2005, a speaking test has been included.
Length & Type - Less than 3 hours
Purpose - Tests English language proficiency in non-native speakers. Colleges often waive TOEFL if you score 75 or above on Regents English
Registration & Fees - www.ets.org/toefl
(800) 468-6335

CLEP (College Level Examination Program)
Length & Type - 1 hour and 30 minutes
Purpose - This test allows students to "place out" of a college class depending on how well they do on the CLEP
Registration & Fees - www.collegeboard.com
(800) 257-9558

Please confirm all information with the organizations listed above.

BOTTOM OF THE NINTH

You've just learned about some of the ways you can improve your profile as you get ready to be a part of the recruiting process. Using the list below, make a note about where you rate in each of these areas, and where you'd like to be. If it's an area that needs improvement, highlight it so you can focus your plan to improve.

	Excellent	**Average**	**Needs Work**	**Goal**
ON THE FIELD				
Leadership	❏	❏	❏	_____
Arm Strength	❏	❏	❏	_____
Foot Speed	❏	❏	❏	_____
Fielding	❏	❏	❏	_____
Hitting	❏	❏	❏	_____
Attitude	❏	❏	❏	_____
Practice Habits	❏	❏	❏	_____
Relationship w/ coach	❏	❏	❏	_____
Relationship w/ team	❏	❏	❏	_____
OFF THE FIELD				
Grades	❏	❏	❏	_____
SAT/ACT Scores	❏	❏	❏	_____
Time Management	❏	❏	❏	_____
Work Ethic	❏	❏	❏	_____
Attitude	❏	❏	❏	_____
Leadership	❏	❏	❏	_____
Involvement/Interests	❏	❏	❏	_____
Volunteer Work	❏	❏	❏	_____
Relationship w/ Counselor	❏	❏	❏	_____
Relationship w/ Teacher	❏	❏	❏	_____

4
YOUR COLLEGE LINEUP

In This Chapter

- How to rank schools by academic factors
- Making sure you will like the campus life
- Reasons to target certain schools
- What to look for in the baseball program
- How to cross-reference your baseball and academic needs and desires

In order to become the focus of a college baseball coach on the hunt for new players, you've got to work hard to make him aware of who you are and what you can do. This chapter is about another step in the recruiting process: Doing the research and investigation required to create a Target List of schools that meet your academic and athletic needs. From your Target List, there will be 5-10 schools you will apply to and one that you may ultimately attend. Coaches from these schools will hear from you, evaluate you at their camps and showcases, and hopefully your high school coach and guidance counselors will reach out to them as well. Ironically, at the beginning of this process, it's you who will be doing the recruiting of the college coach you want to play for.

CREATING YOUR TARGET LIST

STEP 1 - Who Are You?

Let's start by trying to identify the schools that interest you for academic and personal growth reasons. Why start with academics? Because chances are, like 99% of all other college bound high school players, you may not have the good fortune of earning a living playing professional baseball.

 If you want a great online resource for college searching, US News & World Report (www.usnews.com/) offers a fabulous search engine that you should definitely explore.

At the end of your college career, you will leave campus with at least three priceless assets: great memories of college baseball, friends you will have for life, and a diploma. After you've thrown your last pitch, run down your last fly ball and hit your last line drive, your degree, and the education it represents, will be your ticket into the career of your choice and the beginning of your adult life.

We think the best way to begin evaluating schools is to first evaluate yourself. Once you know your own strengths and weaknesses academically, personally and athletically, it will be much easier to match yourself with different colleges. Take out a paper and pen and describe yourself according to these categories:
- Academic likes and dislikes: which subjects do you enjoy the most? What do you want to learn more about? What have you excelled at to date?
- Extracurricular: which recreational activities, community services, and religious activities do you currently participate in and hope to continue in college?
- Personality Traits: are you shy or outgoing? Independent or prefer a structured environment? Want to be far from home or within driving distance? Hang out with different kinds of people?

As we said earlier, "What's the best college for me?" is a multiple-choice question with more than one right answer. What we are trying to help you to do is divide the enormous pie of American colleges into manageable slices, creating boundary lines between broad categories of schools. As long as you focus on the slice with schools that feel right for you, a good choice will be made no matter which school you ultimately select.

Say, for example, you want a medium-sized school with a suburban campus, within driving distance from home, a strong business faculty and a competitive Division II baseball team. There may be up to a dozen schools which fit this criteria, and the differences among them will be much less significant than say, the difference between a big state university and any institution in your target group.

Once you have written down as much information about yourself as possible, it's time to begin looking at schools and learning about which ones look promising and which ones you can eliminate from consideration. Below are the factors which we think work best to quickly screen colleges and enable you to come up with a small but reasonably diverse list of schools which you can then attempt to visit or research in greater depth.

Factor 1 - Location, Location, Location
Just like in real estate, location is an important consideration when trying to whittle down a list of colleges from hundreds to dozens. Schools are either "nearby," "within driving distance," or "a plane ride away." The closer to home you wish to be, the more schools you can cross off your consideration list. Conversely, if you have no preference about distance from home or being far away, then location is less of an issue for you.

Work with your parents on this one because where you go to school obviously has a big effect on how often you will see your family over the next four years, and how often they will see you. There's also a cost element to consider as getting to and from school can be hundreds or even thousands of dollars a year.

Likewise, do you want to be in a rural, suburban or urban setting? On the walk from your dorm to the library, will you encounter shattered glass and boarded-up buildings, or ivy-clad brick buildings and broad expanses of green? During your downtime, will you go snowboarding or snorkeling, apple picking or clothes shopping? Many students also underestimate how strongly the weather can affect their spirits and ability to succeed. If you live in a warm southern climate, love the beach and have never skied before, make sure you understand that going to college in places like New York, Boston or Chicago will require a rather significant lifestyle adjustment.

Factor 2 - Size Matters
The size of a school - how many students and square miles of campus - is also very influential on the quality of your college experience. Big schools with tens of thousands of students are almost like medium-sized cities unto themselves. Do you want to walk to class or take a shuttle bus? Be able to meet in person with your professors after class just to get an e-mail correspondence going? Choose from hundreds of clubs and organizations to join (for example, there are 900 clubs and organizations at the University of Wisconsin-Madison)? The advantages of a big school are many - incredible academic and extracurricular choices, lots of different people from different places to meet and befriend, and well-financed athletic teams and facilities.

You should also keep in mind that local companies tend to recruit on campuses, leading many graduates to settle in the area where they attended college. So quite often, your choice of a college impacts the region you settle in for good, not just for four years.

Depending on your personality, however, you may find these pluses don't outweigh your concerns about large class sizes, the impersonal nature of such a large community, and having to interact with the bureaucracy which manages today's big modern university. Smaller schools, on the other hand, typically have smaller classes, a more intimate social environment, and a generally more accessible administration. Combine your size and location preferences and you probably have made a great start toward narrowing the list of schools you want to spend time researching further.

Factor 3 - Majors Are Minor Issues, For Now
What do you want to major in? It may be the most popular question put to college bound high schoolers as they enter application season. While it's fine, perhaps even an advantage, to know what you want to major in at college, it's also perfectly fine to be undecided. So why bring it up here? Well, if you're one of those young people who know exactly what he wants to study - engineering, hotel and restaurant management, or agricultural science, for example - you certainly will have an easier time creating a list of colleges to focus on.

If you're the opposite type and have no idea what you want to major in, then you probably would want to avoid the specialty schools which means you too can narrow your list. For students in between, who can't specify what they do or don't want to study, don't worry. Most students arrive at school with one major in mind and then decide to switch, sometimes as late as their junior year of college. If you aren't sure what direction to take, just concentrate on schools with lots of options. It's okay to be flexible in life and in college majors!

Factor 4 - Campus Culture
You will do your best academically if you feel like you fit in on campus. Reflect on your social life in high school. Are you looking for a school that offers more diversity? Less? Do you want to spend your nights at film festivals, frat parties or focusing on studies?

During your campus visits, take some time to observe the student body and see how they interact with each other. If you get a chance to talk to students on campus, ask how people with different backgrounds and interests get along. College is an amazing place where you will grow emotionally and intellectually by leaps and bounds. You will have fantastic new experiences in class, with friends and on the field. Only you know which kind of environment suits you best, so be honest with yourself and try to steer toward settings that match up with your comfort zone while still holding out the promise of exciting challenges and opportunities.

Factor 5 - Social and Academic Freedom

Question: "Do you want to go to a college where students are treated like adults, make their own decisions about where to live, which classes to take, and are graded on just midterm and final exams?" Tired of following rules and schedules set by their parents, many college-bound high schoolers would answer with an emphatic "Yes!"

Well, be careful because it's a tricky question. Sudden immersion into a life with few rules isn't always easy. For one thing, if you have freedom, so does everybody else - including the kids who are carousing outside your door the night before your chemistry midterm. Are you the kind of person who is easily influenced by your friends? If the honest answer is yes, then a school with too few rules or a big school where it's easy to get lost in the shuffle may be the wrong place for you.

Colleges differ widely on the matter of how much freedom they grant undergrads. Some schools have lots of detailed rules, like class attendance requirements, designated residential facilities, and restrictions on parties; while others are very hands-off except for extreme behavior such as plagiarism, cheating, or threats to others.

Having thought about whether you would blossom or flounder in an unstructured environment is an important element in the college selection process. Remember, whichever path you choose, you will meet up with hundreds or thousands of young adults who felt the same as you. It would be a shame to arrive at school as a freshman and suddenly discover that you hadn't considered this particular issue carefully enough and were out of sync with your new classmates.

Factor 6 - Religion

This is kind of a subset of Factors 4 and 5 because there are many colleges in America where religion is a central element to campus life and that obviously influences the cultural and academic environment. If you know you want to attend a college with a Catholic, Jesuit, Mormon or Jewish culture, for example, you can narrow your choices to fine institutions like Notre Dame, Loyola, Boston College, Brigham Young, or Brandeis.

If you want the kind of structural, social, and cultural trappings that come with an academic institution that identifies with a particular religion, you are fortunate enough to live in a country where these choices are both available and plentiful. Just do your homework on the schools you are looking at so you know what to expect.

Factor 7 - Diversity

Many colleges, particularly private ones, are making a concerted effort to attract minority students in increasing numbers. If you're going to be a success in the 21st century, you must be capable of understanding and dealing with individuals whose backgrounds are different from yours. It will also make you a better human being.

Guidance counselors caution students to look at more than statistics when considering diversity. They suggest you consider whether the curriculum embraces other traditions and whether residence halls tend to be integrated or segregated. For schools where the commitment to diversity is made in earnest, the opportunity for you to acquire a deeper understanding of others can be a large reward.

Factor 8 - Academic Qualifications

If you are a C student with combined SAT's below 1500, there are many schools you will not qualify for academically, so just scratch them from your list and move on. Not everyone can go to an Ivy League School and not every Ivy League graduate is a success in the adult world. Our point is simple and obvious: be optimistic, but also be realistic.

Take into account the minimum academic performance each school is looking for before you put them on your Target List. This is one of those cold realities of the college selection process. While its fine to have a couple of schools on your Target List that would be considered as "stretches," make sure you also end up with schools where you are well within the range of their academic requirements.

We've listed eight factors that we believe can help you quickly and effectively narrow a huge pool of schools to a Target List of a dozen or so colleges; a group small enough for you to research each institution individually and put them in order of preference. Next is Step 2 where you'll need to evaluate the athletic side of the table to see which of the schools on your Target List also suit your baseball needs.

How Some Schools Stack Up

Aside from choosing a school to play baseball at, you are also choosing a new home. It is important that you are comfortable with all aspects of life on campus. Some criteria to consider include: which schools offer the Best Value, Best Academic Facilities, Best Freshman Housing, Biggest Party School, and What's Hot and Trendy. Here are how some schools stack up, in no particular order, according to Kaplan's book, *The Unofficial, Biased, Insider's Guide to the 320 Most Interesting Colleges*. To order your copy, call 1-800-KAP-TEST or go to www.kaptest.com/

Best Value
Rice U., TX
U. of Kansas, KS
U. of Minnesota, MN
Oklahoma State U., OK
U. of Nebraska, NE
U. of Wisconsin, WI
Texas Tech U., TX
U. of Maryland, MD
Berea C., KY
Penn State U., PA
U. of Virginia, VA
C. of New Jersey, NJ
U. of Arizona, AZ
U. of Michigan, MI
Yale U., CT
West Virginia U., WV
Purdue U., IN
U. of California, CA
U. of Notre Dame, IN
Rutgers U., NJ
U. of Washington, WA
Harvard U., MA
U. of Colorado, CO
U. of Missouri, MO
Truman State U., MO
Virginia Poly & State U., VA
U. of Texas, TX
Duke U., NC
U. of North Carolina, NC
Miami U., OH
Washington U., MO
James Madison U., VA
Cornell U., NY
Stanford U., CA
U. of Delaware, DE
Texas A & M U., TX
Tulane U. LA
Grove City C., PA

Best Academic Facilities
Brown University, RI
Georgetown University, DC
Mass. Inst. Tech., MA
Kenyon College, OF
Pomona College, CA
Columbia University, NY
Lafayette College, PA
Claremont McKenna College, CA
Cooper Union, NY
Bowdoin College, ME
Davidson College, NC
Illinois Wesleyan University, IL
Amherst College, MA
Haverford College, PA
Bucknell University, PA
Emory University, GA
Northwestern University, IL
Cornell University, NY
Colgate University, NY
Cal. Institute of Technology, CA
Carleton College, MN
Bates College, ME
Colby College, ME
Middlebury College, VT
Princeton University, NJ
Dartmouth College, NH
Rice University, TX
Grinnell College, IA
Harvard University, PA
Johns Hopkins University, MD
Duke University, NC
Stanford University, CA
Swarthmore College, PA
The Colorado College, CO
University of Notre Dame, IN
University of Pennsylvania, PA
University of Richmond, VA
Vassar College, NY
Washington and Lee University, VA
Washington University, MO
Webb Institute, NY
Wellesley College, MA
Wesleyan University, CT
Williams College, MA
Yale University, CT

Best Freshman Housing
U. of California, CA
Texas A & M U., TX
Kent State, OH
U. of Texas, TX
Rice U., TX
U. of California, CA
Stephan F. Austin State U., TX
Illinois Wesleyan U., IL
Miami U., FL
Penn State U., PA
Stanford U., CA
Indiana U. of Penn, PA
U. of Central Florida, FL
Florida State U., FL
U. of Utah, UT
Michigan State, MI
Texas Tech U., TX
Wright State, OH
U. of Illinois-Urbana, IL
New York U., NY
Ball State U., IN
Grand Valley State U., MI
Marshall U., WV
Oklahoma State U., OK
Stonehill C., MA
U. of North Carolina, NC
Washington State U., WA

Best Party Schools
Bloomsberg U. of Penn., PA
California State U., CA
East Carolina U., NC
Florida State U., FL
Penn State U., PA
San Jose State U., CA
Southern Illinois U., IL
Southwest Texas State U., TX
SUNY at Albany, NY
U. of Texas, TX
U. of Florida, FL
U. of Georgia, GA
U. of Massachusetts
U. of Miami, MI
U. of Missouri, MO
U. of Virginia, VA
U. of Wisconsin, WI
U. of Wisconsin, WI
Washington State U., WA

Hot & Trendy
New York U., NY
Arizona State U., AZ
U. of California, CA
George Washington U., DC
Pepperdine U., CA
Boston C., MA
Florida State U., FL
Brown U., RI
Stanford U., CA
Duke U., NC
Boston U., MA
San Diego State U., CA
Harvard U., MA
Mass Inst. of Tech., MA
U. of California, CA
Texas A & M U., TX
Penn State U., PA
U. of Arizona, AZ
Princeton U., NJ
Georgetown U., DC
U. of Colorado, CO
U. of North Carolina, NC
U. of Maryland, MD
U. of Southern California, CA
U. of Florida, FL
U. of Texas-Austin, TX
U. of Miami, FL
U. of Virginia, VA
U. of Wisconsin, WI
Virginia Poly Inst., VA
Wash. U. Saint Louis, MO

STEP 2 - Will I Contribute?

Step 2 is to take your Target List and research each school's baseball program. Try to place them in order based on whether you think you have an opportunity to make the team and be a starter. At the top of this list would be schools where you feel you could step right in and play your freshman year. At the bottom of the list would be the schools where you're not sure you would even make the team.

Make sure that you visit www.collegecoachesonline.com every few months and search for schools that meet your criteria. This is an extremely valuable resource that you definitely want to use. A free one-year subscription is included with this guide. Email info@collegeboundsports.com if you misplaced your login password.

Focus On Schools Where You Can Be an Everyday Player
We think it's worth repeating: the most important sports factor to consider in prioritizing your Target List is the likelihood of being an everyday player. Since it could be unlikely you will play professional baseball, what's the point of spending your last four years in the game riding the bench? Instead, play the game you love at a school where you will also receive a solid education.

Be Prepared To Play In Any Division
It's a good idea to include schools from every division (NCAA, NAIA, and NJCAA) on your Target List. Don't get hung up on Division I schools. There are schools at every level that can meet your athletic and education needs. If you are one of those rare birds that has legitimate major league potential, your talent and promise will shine through to scouts no matter where you play. Look at the bios of today's major league and minor league players and you will see the names of colleges you never even heard of before.

Honestly Assess Your Athletic Ability

- Have you received any recognition? All-League? All-County? All-State?
- How have you performed at major events like showcases, tournaments, and national camps
- Do you know any college players with abilities similar to yours?
- Do you possess impressive physical attributes? A coach may recruit you if he believes that you can develop into a great athlete over the next 2-3 years (For example, a 6'5" pitcher with terrible mechanics, but who can throw the ball 87 mph, might catch the eye of a recruiter).
- Do you possess the leadership ability necessary to play in college?
- Do you play on a competitive summer team?

Keep in mind that you may compare yourself to the other athletes on your team, in your league, or to the other athletes you compete against in tournaments and consider yourself a top recruit. Meanwhile, coaches scout not only those same athletes, but also thousands more throughout the country. That's why it's important to attend camps and showcases outside your region.

This reality check is not meant to destroy your dream, just alter it enough to make it more attainable. Remember that each school's needs can change from year to year. A school may have depth in the outfield for the next few years, but have a current need for catchers, left-handed pitchers, and a first baseman. Priorities can change because of graduation, injuries, transfers, sub-par performances, star players leaving college early to play pro ball, or academic suspensions. There is a match for you somewhere in the country. Keep an open mind and do not neglect a school simply because of its name.

Hit the Web
Check out the Media Guides or web pages of your Target List schools. This will give you a feel for how important the athletic department is within the school's hierarchy and how important baseball is within the athletic department. Hopefully, the school's web site will also tell you about the baseball coaches, facilities, and the conference the school competes in. You should also check out the biographies of each player on the roster. It's a pretty good indicator of whether or not the coach recruits athletes like you.

Take into account the following:

Ability
If you notice that most players on a team received All-State accolades during their senior high school season and you've only received All-League Honorable Mention, that's a pretty good indicator that the talent level may be too high for you.

Physical Characteristics
How does your height and weight measure up to other players on the team, especially at your position? If you're a 5'7" pitcher, for example, and the smallest pitcher on the college roster is 6'2", it's easy to surmise that a particular coach recruits tall pitchers.

"Primarily, we recruit in the state of Florida. We hold our baseball camps down here and there is no question, that gives us the opportunity to take a look at high school players up close and personal." - Mike Martin, Head Baseball Coach, Florida State University, NCAA D-I

Geography
Does the coach recruit nationally, regionally or is he satisfied with the in-state talent? Where are most of the athletes from?

Position
How many players are at your position and how many more years of eligibility do they have left? As you know, coaches recruit on need. If there are several returning players at your position (some of whom may be receiving scholarship money), there is a strong chance the coach is going to recruit at other positions, regardless of your ability.

Years of Eligibility
If an underclassman at your position started every game and led the team in batting average, you may have a difficult time breaking into the lineup. A better sign is a team loaded with upperclassmen at your position where the coach is probably looking to replenish the roster.

Playing Time
Try to figure out if anyone on the team started as a freshman. Some coaches have a philosophy that dictates freshman must wait at least a year before becoming a starter.

Junior College Transfers
Does the coach recruit "JUCO" transfers, who generally are more experienced and better athletes than high school graduates?

CASE STUDY: How One Player Used Athletic Team Web Pages to Evaluate Schools for his Target List

Here is how one fictional player - Jason Kline - used the web to compare schools on his Target List. Using his physical attributes and high school statistics, he examined how he fit into two different collegiate baseball programs. Take a similar approach with your search.

PERSONAL INFO

Name: Jason Kline
Height: 5-8
Weight: 150
Position: SS
B/T: R/R
Graduation: 2007
Hometown: Yorktown Heights, NY
School: Yorktown High School

2006 STATS

AVG	GP	AB	R	H	2B	3B	HR	RBI	BB	SO
.325	31	114	28	37	13	4	6	24	14	9

Bio

Jason is an outstanding shortstop entering his second full season on the varsity squad at Yorktown High School. Last year as a junior, Jason led the team in average (.325) and hits (37) and was second in RBI (24). He also led the team in fielding percentage (.977), committing just 1 error in 44 chances at short. Named team captain for his senior year, Jason will make a run at a second consecutive All-Section honor in Westchester County.

Goals

Upon graduation, Jason wants to play for a Division I program on the east coast. He wants the opportunity to start at shortstop and have an immediate impact his freshman year. With this in mind, he's narrowed his Target List down to two schools. Always enamored by the Florida State program, Jason grew up watching the Seminoles compete on television, he's aware of his father's success as the FSU third baseman ('71-'75). He would relish the opportunity to continue his father's legacy in an established collegiate baseball program.

He is also considering Quinnipiac U., a smaller institution located in Connecticut. Quinnipiac is entering its fifth season as a Division I program and Jason sees this as a good place to bring his leadership qualities and grow with the program. Though completely different options, Jason sees advantages to both schools and is ready to "hit the web."

FLORIDA STATE UNIVERSITY'S BASEBALL ROSTER

Overall Record: 54-11-1
League Record: 19-5
National Ranking: #1
Head Coach: Mike Martin

No.	Name	Pos	B/T	HT	WT	YR.	Hometown
1	Tony McQuade	OF	S/R	6-2	205	SO	Gainesville, FL
2	Rocky Roquet	OF	R/R	6-2	195	FR	Anaheim, CA
4	Stephen Drew	SS	L/R	6-0	175	FR	Hahira, GA
5	Jerrod Brown	1B	L/R	5-10	200	JR	Auburndale, FL
7	Daniel Hodges	P	L/L	6-0	180	JR	Hilliard, FL
8	Michael Futrell	OF	R/R	6-0	180	SR	Tallahassee, FL
9	Kevin Richman	SS	S/R	6-0	160	FR	Clearwater, FL
10	Chris Hart	1B	S/R	6-1	190	JR	Clearwater, FL
13	Justin Miller	P	L/L	5-9	150	FR	Quincy, FL
14	Bryan Zech	2B	R/R	5-10	175	SO	Wellington, FL
15	Jeff Probst	2B/SS	R/R	5-10	175	SO	Clearwater, FL
16	Scott Toole	2B/3B	R/R	6-1	185	SR	Jacksonville, FL
17	Chris Whidden	P	R/R	6-0	175	JR	Tallahassee, FL
18	D. Davidson	P	L/L	6-4	215	JR	Panama City, FL
19	A. Cheesman	C	R/R	5-10	190	FR	Sarasota, FL
20	Robinson	OF	R/R	6-1	190	FR	D. Bar, CA
21	Blair Varnes	P	R/R	6-2	200	SR	Pascagoula, MS
22	Jason Newlin	P	R/R	6-0	185	JR	Tallahassee, FL
23	Tony Richie	C	R/R	6-1	210	SO	Jacksonville, FL
24	Eric Roman	P	R/R	6-2	195	JR	Orlando, FL
25	Nick Rogers	OF	R/R	6-1	195	SR	Vedra Beach, FL
26	Kevin Lynch	P/3B	L/R	6-2	185	FR	Ft. Pierce, FL
27	R. Barthelemy	3B/1B	L/R	6-3	230	SR	Miami, FL
29	Richie Smith	OF	L/R	5-11	200	SR	Bristol, FL
30	Robby Read	P	R/R	6-2	195	JR	Tallahassee, FL
31	M. LaMacchia	P	R/R	6-0	190	SO	Palm Harbor, FL
32	Blair McCaleb	C	R/R	6-0	205	SR	Marietta, GA
35	Brent Marsh	P	R/R	6-3	185	FR	Tallahassee, FL
42	Tommy Stewart	OF	R/R	6-2	225	JR	Largo, FL
43	Trent Peterson	P	R/L	6-1	180	SO	Tallahassee, FL
46	Matt Lynch	P	L/L	6-2	185	JR	Ft. Pierce, FL

Relevant Numbers

- 31 players on roster
- 8 freshman
- 6 sophomores
- 10 juniors
- 7 seniors
- 6 of the freshman are position players, 2 pitchers
- 25 are from Florida
- 3 SS on roster: (2 freshman, 1 sophomore)

Look below at Jason's evaluation of Florida State. Remember, this is based on his profile and goals. You may have a different outlook.

Things to consider...

- Nationally recognized as one of country's top programs.
- Incredible facilities, fields, road trips, etc.
- 3 SS on the roster - all are freshman and sophomores so I'd probably need to change positions to have a chance at seeing time.
- Coach recruits primarily from Florida - very few out-of-staters on roster.
- Will have to compete against some of country's top players for a roster spot.
- All players on roster have more accolades than I do.
- All players on roster are taller and heavier than I am.
- Will most likely have to make team as a walk-on.
- Too far for parents/friends to attend my games.
- Would be a dream to experience College World Series and be on ESPN.

QUINNIPIAC UNIVERSITY'S BASEBALL ROSTER

Overall Record: 17-24
League Record: 14-13
National Ranking: #278
Head Coach: Dan Gooley

No.	Name	Pos.	B/T	Ht.	Wt.	YR	Hometown
1	Avery, Keith	OF	R/R	5-10	170	JR	Trumbull, CT
2	D'Elia, Charles	SS	R/R	5-11	165	SR	Neponset, NY
3	Bennett, Dave	P	R/R	6-0	170	SO	Fairfield, CT
4	Puccio, Sal	1B/3B	R/R	6-1	205	SR	Brightwaters, NY
5	Jasilli, John	IF/P	R/R	5-11	155	SR	Brooklyn, NY
7	Marano, Albert	OF	R/R	5-10	170	SO	Lincoln, RI
8	Zides, Andy	IF	R/R	5-8	175	JR	Canton, MA
9	Silverstein, St.	C	R/R	5-8	160	SO	Merrick, NY
10	Bengel, Richard	P	L/L	5-11	175	SO	New Bern, NC
11	Abrahams, Dan	OF	R/R	5-7	140	SO	Great Neck, NY
13	Melillo, John	P	R/R	5-10	190	JR	Wethersfield, CT
14	Garrett, Robert	C/1B	R/R	6-2	200	JR	Brookfield, CT
19	Magee, Brian	OF	L/R	6-2	200	SR	Stamford, CT
20	Spahr, Mike	P	R/R	6-2	205	FR	Oceanport, NJ
21	LaPointe, T.	IF	R/R	6-0	190	JR	West Haven, CT
24	Rankowitz, K.	C	R/R	6-0	185	SO	Barrington, RI
25	Stonaha, Chris	3B	R/R	6-0	175	SO	Stratford, CT
30	Lavigne, Seth	OF	R/R	6-3	240	JR	Tolland, CT
31	Kafka, Ari	P	R/R	6-5	215	FR	Sharon, MA
32	Ellis, Jackson	P	R/R	6-1	190	JR	Ludlow, VT
33	Vartuli, Chris	C	R/R	6-0	190	SO	Norwalk, CT
36	Gresh, Chris	P	R/R	6-1	220	FR	Jewett City, CT

Relevant Numbers

- 22 players on roster
- 3 freshman
- 8 sophomores
- 7 juniors
- 4 seniors
- All 3 freshman are pitchers
- 15 are from NY/CT/NJ
- 1 SS on roster (a senior)

Look below at Jason's evaluation of Quinnipiac. Remember, this is based on his profile and goals. You may have a different outlook.

Things to consider...

- Not known for baseball program.
- Coach recruits from the northeast.
- Small school, less pressure.
- 1 SS on the roster and he's graduating.
- Good chance of seeing a lot of time freshman year.
- Players on roster have accolades more in line with mine.
- Less competition for a starting position.
- Average player on roster is roughly my size.
- School is closer to home so family/friends can watch me play.
- No freshman position players on roster -- may have to wait until sophomore year to start.
- All 3 freshmen on the team are pitchers.
- Smaller roster means fewer spots available, fewer scouts, fewer road trips, etc.
- Cold weather climate - can't play outside year-round.

Final Analysis

You can learn a lot about how you fit in with a particular program just by evaluating their roster on-line. However, a roster from one particular year is not proof of a trend and some media guides inflate the accomplishments of their athletes to make their program appear more prestigious.

As always, the bottom line is that there is no substitute for going the extra step after your initial research is done. Reach out to coaches, players and recent graduates as well as independent sources of statistical information on your Target List schools. Be as knowledgeable as possible on each college you are considering applying to.

Watch for Red Flags

A couple of red flags we need to make sure you are aware of when investigating baseball programs of schools on your Target List. If you notice a team you're interested in has only a few juniors and seniors on the roster, inquire about the following:

- Does the coach bring in more recruits than he needs, only to "weed" them out in the fall?
- How many baseball players receive diplomas?
- Do players suffer an unusually high number of injuries?

STEP 3 - Finalize Your List

You now should have two versions of your Target List, one with schools in order of academic preference and the other in order of baseball preference. See if you can combine the two lists without dramatically changing the order of either one. If one or more of the schools are in the top 10 of both lists, you've got yourself a great indicator of which schools you should focus on applying to and gaining admission.

BOTTOM OF THE NINTH

Okay, you now know how to do it, so it's time to build those lists. Using the information in this chapter, and the information from the previous chapters as well, begin to build your lists of schools based on academics and baseball. Then, compare the two lists, and you've begun to target schools that are a good all-around match for you.

Academic Schools   **Baseball Schools**

_____   _____

_____   _____

_____   _____

_____   _____

_____   _____

_____   _____

_____   _____

_____   _____

_____   _____

_____   _____

_____   _____

_____   _____

_____   _____

5
ESSENTIAL ACTION STEPS TO TAKE

In This Chapter

- Different ways to promote yourself
- How and when to make campus visits
- Information on recruiting services
- When it's a good idea to try out as a walk-on
- Showcase camps you can attend
- How and why to produce a highlight video
- Information on all-star, travel, and select teams

So far in this guide, you've learned how college coaches look at the recruiting process, where you can get help, how to improve your profile to generate interest, and how to make a Target List of colleges you might want to attend. Now, it's time to take action. This chapter will cover a variety of steps you can take to make sure college coaches on your Target List schools are aware of you, take an interest in you, and, as a result, increase your chances of being admitted to the schools of your choice.

PROMOTING YOURSELF

Apply To Strong Academic Schools
As you might suspect, college coaches frequently work with admission officers to get student-athletes admitted who might otherwise not qualify academically or are "on the bubble." Of course, this does not mean a student whose academic profile is significantly below the school's minimums will be accepted simply at the coach's request. However, if you are within a reasonable distance of a school's SAT/ACT and grade requirements, and are a baseball the coach is seeking to add to his squad, the coach probably has a good shot at getting you into his school if he pushes hard enough.

At some schools, admission requirements may not be as stringent for baseball recruits as they are for non-athletes. An Ivy League school may require students to possess at least a 3.6 GPA and a 2100 SAT score, yet a sought-after baseball recruit may only need to have a 3.3 GPA and 1650 SAT. Remember, coaches at strong academic schools seek good players just like their counterparts at the top D-I programs. Their baseball programs have every bit as much tradition and history, sometimes even more than the big D-I baseball schools. And when you graduate, you have an excellent chance of obtaining a great job or being admitted to a graduate school of your choice.

Also, you have a much better chance of playing college baseball by being a big fish in a small pond if you include some smaller or low profile schools on your list. For example, if your Target List features the University of Texas (a national D-I powerhouse) where thousands of players may apply, and Florida's Eckerd College (a lesser-known baseball program, yet an outstanding academic school) where hundreds of athletes may apply, which school do you think gives you a better chance of getting noticed? It's obvious - the statistics favor you at the smaller school.

The bottom line: use the baseball talents you have worked so hard to develop to give yourself a shot at getting accepted to one of the academic "reach" schools on your Target List. You owe it to yourself to pursue the best possible academic education available.

Let Coaches Know You're Interested
During your junior year, send a letter of interest to each head coach on your Target List. The purpose of the letter of interest is to let each coach know that you would like to attend his school for academic reasons and to play for his team.

 If you're not sure how to write your Letter of Interest or Player Profile, there are samples in Chapter 8.

It is extremely important to personalize your letter of interest. If your writing is neat, you might get even more mileage out of a handwritten letter. Make sure you spell the coach's name and address correctly, and include something specific about his team (i.e., last year's win-loss record, top rivals, great facilities) so he knows your interest is based on knowing something about his program.

One cardinal rule, whether your letter is handwritten or printed from a computer, do not send a coach a photocopied letter. How do you feel when you get one of those letters that pretends to be written to just you, when it's obvious that same letter has also been sent to thousands of other people? You feel like the sender has no idea who you are and doesn't really care, right? You want a coach to understand that you have genuine and specific interest in his school and that you have devoted a lot of time to researching his track program. So make each letter of interest an original, from start to finish!

Begin the letter by explaining your interest in the school's academic program. Mention the major you will pursue or ones you are interested in learning more about. Perhaps the school boasts some famous professors whose classes you'd like to attend, or famous graduates who had similar interests to yours.

Discuss your educational and career goals, leadership ability, and your personal values. These characteristics demonstrate to the coach that you are a well-rounded person and that you plan on staying in school all four years. Avoid the temptation to discuss only baseball in your letter. Coaches are impressed by players who treat academics just as seriously as baseball.

But, don't forget to emphasize your baseball accomplishments and why you feel you can contribute to the team.
- Let the coach know that you have a highlight video available if he would like to see you in action.
- Do not send your tape unless a coach specifically asks for it.
- Request literature about the college, a media guide, and a camp and game schedule.
- Mention you'd like to come watch the team play.

Along with your letter of interest, you should also provide your Player Profile, which is discussed below, and a copy of your high school schedule in case the coach decides to send a recruiter to one of your games. Limit your letter of interest to one page (not including the schedule or profile) because coaches are busy people.

Write Your Player Profile
In addition to your upcoming schedule, you should also include a Player Profile of yourself with each letter of interest you send. This one-page résumé should contain personal information, such as your interests, jobs you have held, volunteer or community work you have done, as well as highlights of your academic and baseball accomplishments. See Chapter 8 for details about what items you should include in your Player Profile.

Telephone & E-Mail Contact
After you mail your letter of interest and Player Profile to coaches on your Target List, it is important for you to maintain periodic telephone and/or e-mail contact with the school's baseball department. This will let the coach know that your interest is strong and sincere. It will also give you an opportunity to evaluate where you stand on the recruiting depth chart.

Make sure you have a purpose to each contact with a coach or school. For example, you can inform the coach of a tournament or showcase you are attending, ask questions about the baseball program, request information about the school that cannot be found from published sources, or find out if the coach would like to see your highlight tape. Remember, it is illegal for NCAA coaches to call you or to return your phone calls until July 1 before your senior year, however they can e-mail you anytime.

You are permitted to phone and e-mail the coach as many times as you like. Just use common sense. The last thing you want to do is annoy a coach by calling or e-mailing too often.

One last bit of advice...you should place the phone calls, not your parents. This will demonstrate that you are a mature and responsible young adult who can speak on his or her own behalf.

Develop Your Own Web Site
Once you are a high school junior, you should publish a personal web site to give college coaches an easy and informative way to learn about you and follow your results. It provides recruiters with a free and immediate way of viewing bio info, references, grades, SAT scores, personal statistics, workouts or even your training log.

Go to the baseball web page of each school on your Target List to find the e-mail addresses of the head coach and assistant coaches (some schools have as many as four different coaches and an administrative assistant who handles recruiting). Then e-mail each coach with a link to your web site and invite the coach to visit it periodically. Make sure to update your site frequently to encourage repeat traffic.

You can find the coaches' e-mail addresses using the free subscription you received with this guide to www.CollegeCoachesOnline.com. If you haven't already done so, make sure to set up a free personal web site at a site like www.BeRecruited.com. If you decide to design your own website, here are some things to consider:

Ideas to Improve Your Personal Web Page

- Keep the design and layout simple and easy-to-use. Don't make the coach work too hard to find the necessary information.
- Keep it to one page. Coaches are pressed for time, and too much navigating will keep them from visiting.
- Include both academic and athletic information.
- Update the site regularly to keep it current - at least once a week during your season to update your stats.
- Include at least one picture of you in full uniform, or an action shot.
- If you have the ability to include a short video clip, do it.
- Don't worry too much about fancy graphics. The coach will visit to get information, not be entertained.
- Make sure your game statistics, personal statistics, height and weight, and any other information you provide is accurate.
- Make sure there are no spelling or grammatical errors.
- Don't forget to email coaches to let them know the page is there!

Press Clippings & Awards

Encourage your high school and summer league coaches to submit results and photos to all newspapers in your area. If they don't have the time to do this, ask if you could help out by doing it yourself. When you are mentioned in a newspaper, cut out the article and paste it on a sheet of paper with the newspaper's masthead (name of the paper and publication date found on the front page).

Make enough photocopies for all the schools on your Target List and then go through each article with a yellow marker to highlight wherever your name appears. This will allow the coach to learn about your accomplishments quickly and easily. Then send the article to the coaches at each Target List school with a handwritten cover note saying: "Dear Coach (insert name), I thought you might be interested in seeing this story. I look forward to speaking with you soon."

Questionnaires

Once a coach knows you're interested in his program from your Letter of Interest, three important things will happen:
- Your name will be entered in the team's recruiting database.
- You will receive a questionnaire from the coach.
- You will also receive the materials you requested.

The literature you receive will help you learn more about the school and its baseball program and decide whether to keep the school on your Target List. When your questionnaire arrives, complete it honestly. Avoid the temptation to exaggerate your academic or athletic accomplishments. If a coach discovers inconsistencies (for example, saying you throw 87 mph when you only throw 84 mph), he will remove your name from his recruiting list. Also, let the coach know you are serious about his school by returning the questionnaire as soon as possible. Do not put it off!

 Avoid the temptation to let your parents complete your questionnaires. If a coach notices an adult's handwriting or language on your form, he will assume you lack maturity and responsibility, and that your parents want the opportunity more than you do.

Avoid Rushing To Judgment
Do not reject a school too early in the process. Wait until you have thoroughly researched all of your options before telling a coach that you are or are not interested in his school. It's difficult to predict how the recruiting process will evolve, and an offer you turned down in August may be your best or only option in April. Fill out and return everything! If a coach makes the effort to contact you, respond promptly. Don't burn any bridges.

Emphasize Your Unique Selling Point
Although they hate to admit it, many selective colleges target certain groups of applicants for admission. They might want to increase the diversity of the student body, expand the physics department, or recruit a few potential future donors. To have the freshmen community they want, colleges need musicians and athletes, leaders in publications and student government, a certain percentage of alumni children, minorities, and international students. Students in the targeted groups may have an easier time getting through the admissions process, and there is often special scholarship money available for people from certain backgrounds or who are interested in specific programs. You should emphasize what is unique about you.

Prove How Badly You Want To Attend the School
Every time you visit a campus, meet an alumnus, or e-mail a professor, let the admissions office know. By rejecting students who have failed to show genuine interest, colleges can boost the percentage of accepted applicants who enroll. A high percentage of accepted applicants who enroll make schools appear more attractive, and it saves the cost of recruiting students and of "wooing" desirable students with generous merit aid.

A Strong Essay Can Make the Difference
Admissions deans often push hard for the writers of their favorite compositions. On the other hand, they also note the papers that are riddled with typos or grammatical errors. Generally speaking, typos reflect sloppiness. Even if you do have a tendency to be light on the spell check key, there is no excuse for these kinds of errors. They can be eliminated entirely by careful and repetitive proofreading. Eliminate the mistakes and show you care about how you are perceived. Choose a topic you feel passionate about. Be creative!

On-Campus and Alumni Interviews Matter
Interviews are the only personal interaction in an otherwise paper-driven process. Admissions committees frequently consider whether or not you bothered to set this up, and what the interviewer thought of you. Aggressively seek out any official or unofficial representatives of your Target List schools. You never know which contact you make will be the one that will move your application from the "Rejected" to "Maybe" to "Accepted" category.

Take Advantage of Family Ties
If you have siblings, parents, uncles, aunts, or grandparents who attended a school on your Target List, give that institution careful consideration because you have an edge there. Schools generally look favorably on relatives of students and/or alumni for obvious reasons - financial support, spirit, tradition, etc. - and this may give you a leg up over non-affiliated student-athletes who apply. Also, make sure to inform coaches if your father or any of brothers have played college or pro ball.

Get Recommendations
Since most college coaches on your Target List are not going to see you play in person, they will have to rely on recommendations from people they trust. It is extremely important to develop a network of credible and

influential people who will provide recommendations. We recommend you ask the following people whom you know, or may come into contact with, to write and/or call the college coaches on your Target List:
- High school coach
- Opposing high school coaches
- Any college coach, pro scout, or current or former pro player
- Umpires
- Summer league coaches
- Academy directors
- Influential alumni
- Showcase directors/organizers
- Teammates who have gone on to compete in college

This is no time to be shy! Many adults are happy, if not flattered, to be asked to advocate for a young person who has taken the time to respectfully request their assistance. So ask. As we are sure you have heard many times before, the worst thing they can say is no.

When you ask people to write or call a college coach on your behalf, make sure they support you and feel you are college baseball material. The same goes for high school teachers, counselors, and others whom you may ask to write letters of recommendation for you. Choose them carefully. Even one negative comment can be the "kiss of death."

Communicate and be humble!

The best way to communicate with coaches is by phone and in-person. You should do mos of the talking. Coaches like to judge how humble you are and how you treat the "little" people like weaker teammates, janitors, secretaries, etc.

What You See is What You Get
Gregory Collins, Kingston, RI

From day one, I knew it was going to be difficult. In high school, I didn't get the opportunity to play on the varsity team until my junior year. Unfortunately, I was a first baseman at a time when my school was stocked at the position. I mostly sat in favor of my friend, Jay. He was an All-County recipient who happened to be in the same grade. With no opportunity to start at what I felt was my best defensive spot, coach gave me the chance to play third, but it didn't feel right. I would have been the starting first baseman at any other school in our league, but it wasn't meant to be. I felt suffocated.

I had dreams of playing college ball, but was afraid no coaches would give me a look due to my lack of playing time. I wanted to let college coaches see me in action at first base so I decided to create my own highlight video. The results could not have been better. I shot myself hitting, fielding, throwing and running the 60-yard dash. I even played a little third base in the video to show some versatility. It didn't matter that I only had 37 AB all season - with this highlight tape, I had a valuable sample of my talent to show off.

I sent the tape to eight college coaches and heard back from five. They all said my situation was common and that I shouldn't worry because if I had talent, coaches would find me. I wasn't going to wait around for that to happen. I made sure I was seen, and making a highlight video was the perfect way to do it. One of the five coaches who responded ended up being my college coach for four year - I even got to start at first base during my junior and senior seasons.

GOING ON CAMPUS VISITS

Start Early
While campus visits are primarily junior and senior year events, there's no need to wait. Start visiting colleges as early as ninth grade. Take advantage of any chance to walk around a college campus. Check out schools in or near your hometown, stop by colleges during family trips, and visit older friends and siblings at school. The more visits you make, the better you will become at quickly sizing up a school, and recognizing what you want from a college.

"You should narrow your choices to a few schools and then go on recruiting visits. Try and get as much information as you can, and get a feel for the school's atmosphere. In the end, go where you feel comfortable." - Scott Autrey, Pitcher, Hudson Valley Renegades (Tampa Bay Devil Rays Class A Affiliate)

Unofficial Visits
Starting in your freshmen year of high school, you should take unofficial visits to a variety of schools. Even though you are responsible for paying all of the travel expenses, it's a great way to get a good read on a school so you'll feel more confident when you develop your Target List a couple of years later. Make sure to let the baseball coach know you are coming and that you want to stop by to introduce yourself. By making these visits regularly, you'll make a lasting and positive impression on the coaches whose help you may need come application time.

Official Visits
Coaches extend official visit invitations to their top recruits so they can get to know the athletes better and promote their school's best features. Since official visits are an expense for the baseball program, only a limited number of athletes will receive these invitations. If you're fortunate enough to receive one in your junior or senior year, it's an outstanding opportunity for you to evaluate everything about the college and determine if the school and team fit your needs. Most of the time, you will stay in a baseball player's dorm and eat meals with him. This gives you an excellent opportunity to ask lots of questions. Keep in mind:
- The NCAA allows you one expense-paid visit to five different schools. This restriction applies even if you are being recruited in two sports.
- Each visit may only last a maximum of 48 hours.
- You must provide college authorities with your official transcript and entrance exam scores.
- You may return to one of the schools you've already visited, but you must pay all expenses.
- You must be registered with the NCAA Clearinghouse for official visits to NCAA schools.

Pre-Plan Your Schedule
For unofficial visits, call the admissions office at least two weeks in advance to let them know you are coming to campus. An admissions counselor can tell you the dates and times for campus tours (they're usually held weekly), information sessions (a Q & A with an admissions office rep that takes place before the tour), and open houses (a day of events aimed at prospective students, scheduled once or twice a semester). The counselor can also recommend classes to observe, help schedule individual meetings with faculty and coaches, provide out a campus map, a parking permit, and information on nearby lodging.

When to Go
The best time to visit is on a weekday in either semester - not too close to the beginning of the semester and definitely not during finals week. That way, you'll see students and teachers going about their regular routines. For some families, however, a weekend, summer, or winter break visit may be easier to schedule.

While you obviously won't see an average day during those off times, you can still get a sense of the campus and the area. On a blitz tour of schools in a particular region, don't try to cram in more than two schools a day. It takes at least half a day to get an accurate feel for a campus, and, frankly, we think one school a day is a more appropriate pace.

Before Your Visit

Prior to your arrival, learn everything you can about the school. Read the school catalog and browse its web site. Think of questions to ask that are not answered in published materials. (In other words, don't ask, "How many students go to school here?" Instead, ask questions like "What percentage of freshmen drop out?" and "How do you help students in danger of failing?").

Decide beforehand what's important to you - anything from a strong political science department to single-sex dorms to a campus choir. Make a list of priorities and investigate them during your visit. Keep notes and try to ask the same questions at each school so you will have a means to compare them against each other.

What to Do On Campus

- Begin your visit with an information session and a campus tour.
- Sit in on a class.
- Check out the dorms.
- Eat in the cafeteria.
- Read the bulletin boards.
- Meet a faculty member and the baseball coach.
- See the drama or computer or gym facilities
- Read the student newspaper.
- Try to find your favorite book on the library's computer system and then look for it in the stacks.

Remember to check out the area surrounding campus, too. What restaurants, stores, and recreation attractions are nearby? How close is the bus or train station? Think about what you'd need to live around there: A bike? A car? Warmer clothes?

If you visit with your parents, split out at some point so you can roam the campus alone for a taste of what it would be like on your own in this new place. Parents can use this time to meet with a financial aid officer.

Also, make sure to check out the baseball facilities. Stand at your position on the field and in the batter's box Look around. Does it excite you? And by all means, watch the team practice or play a game and see if you can visualize yourself as a member of this team.

Interviews

Some schools offer an interview with an admissions counselor as part of the campus visit. When you call the admissions office, ask if a personal interview is an option. If you have an interview, don't be nervous. The interview is mostly just a chance for you to ask questions of a school official and show that you are interested.

It's also an opportunity to make a positive impression on someone who may decide to go to bat for you in the applications process so make sure you're prepared, respectful, neat, and ask lots of questions. Make sure that you dress nicely as this will make you look mature and respected. Also, make sure you do some research about the school and have specific questions to ask. They will take you seriously if you already have knowledge and show you really want to be there. Some other hints that will help: make sure that you are on time or a little early, make eye contact throughout the interview and be passionate when you speak.

Keep a Notebook Just For College Visits

Take notes while you're on campus, jotting down the name of the dorm you walked through, the class you visited, and the names of professors and students you met (and their phone numbers, so you can call back with follow-up questions). After each visit, write down your impressions - what you did and did not like about the school. Take photos, especially if you visit during junior year, to help you remember each campus months later when you're deciding where to apply. Make sure to write thank you notes to any school official who met with you individually.

Improper Recruiting Danger Signs

Most college baseball coaches have your best interest at heart. However, you should be aware of improper recruiting tactics. Think twice if a coach:

- Tells you that your scholarship commitment is four or five years. Even though most coaches will renew your scholarship each year, they can only promise it one year at a time.
- Guarantees you an easy academic schedule and shows little interest in you as a student.
- Puts you in contact with a booster from the athletic department.
- Speaks negatively about other colleges you're considering.
- Offers you any monetary inducement, including college shirts or souvenirs.

Be sure to speak with your high school coach if you are concerned about any awkward situation. Do not jeopardize your eligibility by ignoring or sweeping it under the rug.

Sample Questions to Ask Athletes on the Team

- How do you like the coaches?
- Is it difficult keeping up with your schoolwork?
- How much time do you devote to the team in the off-season?
- What don't you like about the program?
- How accessible are the academic tutors?
- How are the living arrangements?
- If you could do it all over again, would you still choose this school?
- Do all the baseball players hang out together?
- How many hours per day do you study?
- What do you do socially?
- How do the professors treat baseball players during the season?
- How do the other students on campus feel about baseball players?

Sample Questions to Ask the Baseball Coach

- Are you interested in recruiting me or will I have to walk-on? (Avoid the temptation to ask the coach if he is going to offer you a scholarship. If the coach is interested in you, he will bring it up. It's similar to going to a job interview. Would your first question be, "How much are you going to pay me?" Of course not!).
- What is the policy for walk-ons?
- What position do you see me playing?
- What is the off-season workout schedule?
- Will you red-shirt me?
- If I suffer an injury, become academically ineligible, or you decide I'm just not good enough for the team, what happens to my scholarship, if I have one?
- What are the graduation rates for athletes on the team?

- Am I eligible for any other sources of financial aid?
- Are there academic tutors available?
- How many athletes are on the roster? Are their backgrounds similar to mine?
- Does the team take any special trips?
- How many other players are you also recruiting at my position? Have any of them committed to you yet?
- Is there a specific coach who works with players at my position?
- Are there any team rules or policies I need to be aware of?
- What's my potential of receiving playing time my freshman year?
- Will I have required study hall hours?
- How often does the team lift weights and condition?
- Is this a full year commitment or can I play other sports?

Questions To Ask Yourself After the Visit

- Did the coach have bad things to say about the other schools that are recruiting me?
- Would I attend this school if I had no intention of playing baseball there?
- Do the coaches and athletes get along and respect one another?
- Will I be successful academically at this school? Athletically? How do I measure up to everyone else?
- Were the coaches and players I met honest, friendly, and interested in me, or did they seem to fake it?
- Did the coaches stress academics? Did they ask me about my educational and career goals? Were they knowledgeable about my area of study? If not, did they introduce me to someone to answer my questions?
- Did I respect the coach and his philosophy?
- Will I fit in at this particular school?
- Do I have what it takes to commit to this coach and team for four years?
- Does the school satisfy all requirements that I identified earlier with my parents and counselor?

HIRING RECRUITING SERVICES

Why Recruiting Services May Not Be Effective

For a fee ranging from a couple hundred dollars to over $1,000, you can pay to have a recruiting service promote you to college coaches. They usually send a one-page profile and a highlight video to every school they feel is a good match. This could be several hundred schools or every school in the country.

The problem that coaches find with most recruiting services is that the person doing the evaluating is not credible, nor is it someone they personally know or respect. The evaluators tend to exaggerate your ability and project what level you can play ball at by classifying you as a D-I, D-II, D-III or pro prospect.

Categorizing athletes like this is flawed because the level of play at each school varies so much within each division. In addition, the services bulk mail these profiles, so they are not personalized. This can be annoying for coaches.

Coaches feel some of these services can be a waste of money and that they take advantage of athletes. It's your job to do comprehensive research. Understand that receiving questionnaires or camp invitations from coaches after using a recruiting service does not necessarily mean you are being recruited. Ask questions like the ones below before you commit financially.

Sample Questions to Ask The Recruiting Service Before You Sign Up

- Who evaluates me and does he have a financial interest in how he rates my skills? In other words, is he a salesman or a scout? (An unbiased evaluation has the most credibility with coaches.)
- Can you guarantee me a scholarship? (This is impossible to do.)
- Can anyone use this service or do you have to possess the ability to play collegiate baseball? (The best services only accept athletes with college potential.)
- Can you provide the names and phone numbers of three athletes from my area who have used your service?
- What percentage of the athletes who use your service receive interest from college coaches?
- Have any coaches offered scholarships to athletes as a result of your service?
- Will you send my profile and video in its own envelope? (If it's sent with hundreds of others, it will not get the attention it deserves.)
- How many athletes receive no response even after all your promotion? (An honest service will tell you that most athletes do not receive interest from college coaches.)
- Do you offer a money-back guarantee?
- Which college coaches endorse your service?

What To Look For When Selecting A Recruiting Service

Choosing the right recruiting service to represent you to college coaches could mean the difference between continuing your baseball career or hanging up your spikes for good. Here are five criteria you should consider when choosing a company:

1. Evaluators

Who is grading your skills? It is extremely important that a knowledgeable and respected coach writes your evaluation.

2. Business History
How long has the company been in business? Are they an unproven start-up or have they been around for a while?

3. Enrollment Procedure
Does the company represent any athlete who will pay their fee, regardless of ability? Make sure the service you choose limits enrollment to only athletes with college potential.

4. References
Are they willing to provide names of athletes' parents you can call who have used their service in the past? If not, look elsewhere.

5. Track Record
How many of their past customers play college baseball? Did any receive baseball scholarships? Also, don't be impressed by their All-American alumnus who signs with Florida State. Blue chippers are going to receive attention regardless of the recruiting service.

TRYING TO MAKE THE TEAM AS A WALK ON

What Is A Walk-On?
A walk-on is a term used for a player who does not receive a baseball scholarship but impresses the coaching staff during tryouts and makes the final roster.

Purpose of the Tryout
While it's true that most coaches have a good idea of which players will comprise their final roster before their season begins, open tryouts are necessary for several reasons:
- Each season, a coach is faced with the challenge of fielding the best possible team with only a limited number of baseball scholarships available. An invitation to try to join the team as a walk-on gives the coach some added leverage to lure talented players to his school.
- Every so often, a player who has escaped notice, for one reason or another, gains admittance to the college, shows up at the tryout, impresses the staff, makes the team, and becomes a key contributor. Sometimes, he even ends up with a scholarship in later years.
- Frequently, players get hurt, transfer, leave school early to play professionally, become academically ineligible or drop out of school and the coach must fill their roster openings. If these openings occur after all scholarship money has been awarded, then the coach must rely on the tryout to complete his squad.
- Coaches feel it is a necessary courtesy to offer the sons of influential alumni or important donors a chance to make the team. Although the walk-on invitation is at first a compliment to these players, most of them will probably get cut.
- Most athletic departments require the coach to provide every student an opportunity to make the team.

Odds May Be Against You
Your chances of making a college baseball team as a walk-on are slim. Your chances of seeing considerable playing time if you do make the team are even slimmer. This is especially true at a high-profile D-I school. Coaches invest a lot of time and money in their current crop of recruits and make up the roster well before the tryout. It may be better for you to accept a small scholarship or invitation to a lesser baseball school or a junior college than to try to walk-on at a bigger school. Riding the bench throughout your college career will lead to a miserable athletic experience. Instead, choose a school that gives you a chance to contribute on the field.

When You Should Attempt to Walk-On
You should feel confident in your decision to walk-on if you have been encouraged by the coach to try out (coaches call this player a "recruited walk-on"), seen the college team play several times (either in person or on TV), and you are confident you possess the talent necessary to make the team. It helps if non-biased coaches, scouts, and especially the head coach of the actual team confirm your belief. Some small, low-profile baseball teams do not recruit much at all and rely almost entirely on open tryouts to fill their rosters. Also, and more importantly, make sure you would be happy at the school and be willing to remain there for four years even if you get cut from the team and are unable to play baseball.

Getting a Better Look
If you're a "recruited walk-on," meaning the coaching staff has specifically asked you to come try out for the team and even implied you will make it, you will have a much better opportunity than the "uninvited" player, or the one who just shows up without being the recipient of genuine interest beforehand. Also, if your high school coach has a good relationship with the college coach (either by providing honest evaluations of potential recruits or by encouraging his top players to attend the college), you'll probably receive a better look that most tryout attendees.

ATTENDING SHOWCASES

Showcases are usually one or two-day events that attract about 100 or more players who all desire to play college baseball. Coaches and pro scouts from the region are invited to attend the pro-style workouts and evaluate each player's offensive and defensive skills.

Most coaches are not allowed to communicate with players or parents at the event and they usually stand behind the backstop with a radar gun and stopwatch. Usually, all of the coaches watch one player perform a task (i.e. running, fielding, batting) at a time. This makes showcases outstanding opportunities for exposure.

While every player's ultimate goal is an baseball scholarship, keep in mind that a showcase is only one step in a long recruiting process. Very rarely will a coach make an offer to a player after seeing him at one event. The best time to start attending showcases is during your sophomore or junior year of high school. This gives coaches a chance to follow your progress through high school if you impressed them, and it gives you valuable experience in a tryout environment.

"I get about 150 letters each year and I can't go through them all. I like to see each player compete myself. In that respect, the showcases are great because it helps to cut through a lot of the fat. Occasionally, we do miss top players. However, in this day and age, with all those showcases, you would have to be at the North Pole for us not to find you." - Jeff Albies, Head Baseball Coach, William Patterson U., NCAA D-III

Purpose of the Showcase
College coaches like to recruit at showcases because they can:
- Evaluate many athletes in a short amount of time, especially those that have shown a genuine interest in attending their school.
- Save money - showcases are cost-effective and allow coaches to consolidate their recruiting trips.

You Should Attend Showcases Because You Can:

- Be seen in action by many coaches at one time.
- Evaluate how your ability compares to others from your region.
- Get an unbiased and professional opinion of your ability. After the showcase, make sure to ask the director for your running, fielding, and batting scores.
- Determine your "recruitability." You will know you made an impression if you receive letters or phone calls from coaches who attended the showcase a few weeks later.
- Receive experience competing in a pressure-filled environment. The more showcases you attend, the calmer and more relaxed you will be when they really count (during the summer and fall of your senior year).

Evaluation Format
A typical showcase features a pro-style evaluation that typically includes:
- Running: Timing everyone in the 60-yard dash
- Pitchers: Throwing five fastballs, three curve balls, and two changeups.
- Middle Infielders & Third Basemen: Fielding 4 grounders from deep shortstop and throwing to first base
- First Basemen: Fielding four ground balls from first base and throwing across the diamond to third.
- Outfielders: Fielding four pop flies or ground balls from deep right field, throwing two to third base and two home.

- Catchers: Catching four pitches and throwing them to second base as if a runner was stealing.
- Hitters: 10 swings off a pitcher throwing at BP speed
- Sometimes, informal games are played so coaches can watch players in game situations.

Questions To Ask the Showcase Director Before Registering

- Which coaches have committed to attend? (The biggest problem with showcases is that it's hard to predict exactly which coaches will show up since they are not paid to be there.)
- Which coaches have attended the event during the last two years?
- How many players will attend the showcase?
- What is the format?
- How many players in the past have received interest or scholarships from coaches as a result of attending the showcase?
- Will I play in a game? If yes, how many innings and at-bats can I expect?
- Do you provide references? (If he does, make sure to call them!)
- Is there a refund in case of rain?
- Will I receive college or pro instruction at the event?

Follow-Up With Coaches

You may want to e-mail the coaches who attended the showcase and ask for their advice regarding what areas of your game need improvement and what kind of schools might need a player of your ability. Most coaches, regardless of their recruiting interest in you, will have notes from the showcase rating your running, arm strength, hitting, and fielding ability on a 1-5 pro scale. You never know who can help you. The more people you ask, the more opportunities you will have. Be aggressive!

What Not To Expect

College coaches will probably not do any of the following things at a showcase:
- Announce themselves. Most coaches like to remain anonymous to prevent awkward conversations with players and parents.
- Offer you a scholarship at the event. The showcase is only one step in a long evaluation process.
- Expect you to perform perfectly. In fact, they want to see how you react after you boot a ground ball or strike out. Coaches are there to evaluate your skills and project what level they feel you could play at in two or three years.
- Treat you any differently because of your past accomplishments. Everyone gets the same opportunity to shine.
- Talk to you or your parents. If coaches are interested in you, they will follow up with a phone call or letter.

Tips for Making the Most of Your Showcase Experience

Inform Coaches That You Are Attending the Showcase

Write or e-mail coaches on your Target List, as well as coaches expected to attend and tell them you will be participating in the showcase. Even if some of the schools on your list are located far away, the coaches may want to inform their local scouts to stop by and check you out.

Dress In a Full Uniform

It is important that you look like ballplayer. Make sure to wear a jersey with your name on the back so it is easy for a coach to identify you from the 100 or so other players attending. First impressions are crucial so wear a clean uniform, tuck your jersey in, wear your hat with the bill forward, and leave the jewelry at home.

Hustle
Run at all times, even if others walk. You never know who is watching.

 "The players we recruit have to keep their grades up and make sure to sprint on and off the field. Something as simple as that can be impressive. It makes us aware that the player has a passion to play and succeed. It also lets us know that they want to win as much as we do. Obviously the player needs talent, but hustle will get you far." - Jim Brady, Head Baseball Coach, University of Missouri-St. Louis, NCAA D-II

Get Evaluated At Multiple Positions
Ask to be evaluated at every position that you play well. This will give coaches a chance to see more of you during the day. Also, you may think your primary position is shortstop but a coach may see more potential for you as an outfielder. You are a more attractive recruit if you are versatile enough to play different positions.

Spend Every Minute of Downtime Wisely
Since only one person is evaluated at a time, you will spend a lot of time on the sidelines waiting for your turn. If a coach is interested in you, he may want to keep an eye on you during these times. Don't fool around on the sidelines with your friends. Instead, if it is allowed, use the downtime to practice. You will give interested coaches another opportunity to scout you. When you're on the field, never sit with your butt on the ground. Always take a knee and hustle at all times. There are also coaches, recruiters and scouts who will observe players arriving in the parking lot to get an idea of their attitude. They will observe the player's dress-shirt tucked in neatly, hat not on backwards, etc.-and they will also make negative notes if the player has his parents run errands for him or acts disrespectful. Carry your own equipment-don't have your parents do it.

Cheerlead
If someone makes a great play or need some encouragement, it's okay to cheer him on. Coaches will be impressed by your team spirit and leadership ability.

Leave the Wood at Home
Since you will hit the ball more powerfully and farther with aluminum, why would you choose to bat with wood? It will make you look like a weaker hitter compared to your peers, if you hit with wood and everyone else uses aluminum. While it's true that pro scouts may like to see how you handle a wood bat, almost all college teams still use aluminum.

Get Dirty
Coaches love to recruit players who are not afraid to dive after ground balls or pop flies.

If No Coach Shows Interest In You
Do not assume that just because none of the attending coaches expressed interest in you after the showcase that you cannot play at the college level. Keep this in mind:
- Most coaches attend showcases with specific recruiting needs in mind (i.e. lefty pitchers who throw at least 78 mph or outfielders who run the 60 in 7.1 seconds). The coaches in attendance might not have a need for a player at your position.
- Coaches could be extremely impressed with your ability, but notice your GPA and test scores are too low. In this case, they cross you off their list, no matter how good you are.
- The coaches who attended the showcase are only a very small sample of college baseball. Remember, there are 1,343 teams in the United States.
- There are lots of other showcases to attend. The more coaches that see you play, the better chance you will have of generating interest.

When you are at a showcase, your every move is being evaluated. Here are some things that you should avoid:
- Arriving late.
- Acting like you're a star or big man on campus.
- Wearing your hat backwards.
- Asking your parent to carry your bags or get you water.
- Wearing earrings, bracelets, a watch, or a pony-tail.
- Getting upset if you don't perform well.
- Asking the showcase evaluators your times and rankings before the event is over.
- Not listening to where you're supposed to be.
- Complaining or speaking negatively within earshot of anyone you don't know.

The Showcase Showdown
Joshua Lyons, Ft. Lauderdale, FL

It's not necessarily who you know, but rather, who knows you that's important. This is the mentality I took when deciding to showcase my talent for college coaches and recruiters. True, my .417 BA and 14 HR during my junior year of high school spoke for itself, but I needed to do more. I knew what my potential was, and now it was time for college coaches to find out for themselves. Attending a few showcases was the answer.

I suited up for two showcases here in Florida, and made the trip to North Carolina for another - we take family vacations there every year so it worked out nicely.

I was pretty nervous for the two local showcases, but I calmed down and played really well up north. However, in Florida, I got the chance to see how I compared to other kids from my area. Plus, with many top coaches and scouts in attendance, I got great exposure.

When I got back from North Carolina, there were letters and phone messages waiting from coaches who saw me play in Florida. It was nice to have coaches show interest in me rather than the other way around.

Eventually, I accepted an offer from a coach who saw me play here in Florida. He knew I was going to North Carolina and had another coach follow me there. He was impressed with my effort when he first saw me and wanted another opinion. I didn't even know he was sending someone to scout me. I guess you never know who is watching.

Upcoming Showcases
Listed on the next few pages is a comprehensive roster of showcases throughout the country. While we have every reason to believe that each showcase can be a valuable asset in the selection process, be aware that some may be better than others in your particular circumstances. Do your homework or it could get very expensive! Talk to the organizers, get input from your high school coach and summer league coach, ask the coaches at the schools on your Target List which ones they will attend and which ones have value, and contact any college players from your area to learn which events they attended.

3&2 High School Showcase
PO Box 14011
Lenexa, KS
Director: Jeff Chalk

Web: www.3and2baseball.com
E-mail: kentrettig@3and2baseball.com
Fax: 913-888-6712
Phone: 913-888-8055

Aldrete Baseball Academy
PO Box 4042
Monterey, CA 93942

Phone: 831-884-0400

All American Talent Showcases
6 Bicentennial Ct.
Erial, NJ 08081
Director: Joe Barth

Web: www.thehitdoctor.com
E-mail: hitdoctor@thehitdoctor.com
Fax: 856-354-0818
Phone: 856-354-0201

All Star Baseball Academy
650 Parkway Blvd.
Broomall, PA 19008

Web: www.allstarbaseball.com
E-mail: mman475361@aol.com
Phone: 610-355-2411

Apache Baseball Showcase
PO Box 173324
Arlington, TX

Email: metro500@swbell.net
Phone: 817-492-0965

Area Code Games
PO Box 213
Santa Rosa, CA 95402
Director: Coach Williams

Web: www.studentsports.com
E-mail: rwilliams@areacodebaseball.org
Fax: 707-525-0214

Baseball Factory
9176 Red Branch Road, Suite M
Columbia, MD 21045
Director: Steve Sclafani

Web: www.baseballfactory.com
E-mail: moreinfo@baseballfactory.com
Fax: 410-715-1975
Phone: 800-641-4487

Best of the West Showcase
7515 Vista Alegre St., NW
Albuquerque, NM 87120
Director: Darell Carillo

Web: www.bestofthewestbaseball.com
E-mail: ddc@bestofthewestbaseball.com
Fax: 505-836-1065
Phone: 505-833-0745

Best in Virginia
PO Box 400839
Charlottesville, VA 22904-4839

Web: www.vabaseballcamps.com
E-mail: dkw3b@virginia.edu
Phone: 434-982-5775

College Baseball Coaches Camp
Staffed by college coaches
Long Island, NY
Director: Wayne Mazzoni

Web: www.CollegeBaseballCoachesCamp.com
E-mail: Wayne@WayneMazzoni.com
Phone: 203-260-4932

College Select
PO Box 783
Manchester, CT 06040
Director: Tom Rizzi

Web: www.collegeselect.org
E-mail: TRhit@msn.com
Phone: 800-782-3672

Doyle Baseball Showcases
PO Box 9156
Winter Haven, FL 33833-9156

Fax: 860-645-1067
Web: www.doylebaseball.com
E-mail: scgines@dwu.edu
Fax: 863-439-7086 Phone: 863-439-1000

East Coast Professional Showcases
601 S. College Road
Wilmington, NC 28403
Director: Mark Scalf

Web: www.anglefire.com/dc/eastcoast
E-mail: heyandy@hotmail.com
Phone: 910-962-3570

EJ Sports Showcases
PO Box 2989
San Ramon, CA 94583

Web: www.ejsports.com
E-mail: erik@ejsports.com
Phone: 925-735-2350

Joe Wladyka's Showcases
7 Wilson Ave.
Rutherford, NJ 07070

Phone: 201-935-3917

Mark Cresse Baseball
33-700 Date Palm Drive
Cathedral City, Ca 92234

Web: www.bigleaguedreams.com
E-mail: jeffo@bigleaguedreams.com
Phone: 760-324-5600

Mid America Five Star Showcase
10701 Plantside Drive
Louisville, KY 40299
Director: John Marshall

Web: www.championsbaseball.com
E-mail: champ8@aol.com
Fax: 502-261-9278
Phone: 502-261-9200

Midwest Prospects Showcase
4107 Northwest 50th
Oklahoma City, OK 73112
Director: Brian Rupe

Web: www.midwestprospects.com
E-mail: midwestprospects@aol.com
Phone: 405-942-5455

Metro Showcases
984 Aspen Valley Ave.
Las Vegas, NV 89123
Director: Rich Santigate

E-mail: maureen@alternativa-images.com
Phone: 888-818-0044

Ohio Buckeye Scout Showcase
PO Box 1604
Brentwood, TN 37024
Director: Jeff Fisher

Web: www.ohiobaseball.rivals.com
E-mail: fish71396@aol.com
Phone: 615-507-1010

Perfect Game USA
1203 Rockford Rd SW
Cedar Rapids, IA 52404
Director: Jeery Ford

Web: www.perfectgame.org
E-mail: services@perfectgame.org
Fax: 319-298-2924
Phone: 319-298-2923

Pioneer Valley Charity Showcase
248 Conway St.
Greenfield, MA 01301

Web: www.eteamz.com/pioneervbaseball/
E-mail: peloquin@valinet.com
Fax: 413-775-1707 Phone: 413-775-9040

Premier Baseball Showcase
2411 Teal Ave.
Sarasota, FL 34232

Web: www.premier-baseball.com
E-mail:webmaster@premier-baseball.com
Fax: 941-371-0917   Phone: 941-371-0989

Pro-Motion Sports Blue Grey Classic
83 East Bluff Road
Ashland, MA 01721
Director: Gus Bell

Web: www.impactprospects.com
E-mail: gus@impactprospects.com
Phone: 508-881-2782

Pro Select Baseball
PO Box 36
Franklin Lakes, NJ 07417
Director: Jeery McMahon

E-mail: ProSelectBB@aol.com
Phone: 201-337-7440

Rockland County Showcases
2 Medford Place
Nanuet, NY 10954

E-mail: sigillojr@aol.com
Phone: 914-623-7054

Ron Golden's Baseball Showcase
PO Box 09446
Columbus, OH 43209
Director: Ron Golden

E-mail: RonGolden@compuserve.com
Phone: 614-236-8141

SelectFest Baseball
60 Franklin Place
Morris Plains, NJ 07950
Directors: Bruce Shatel & Brian Fleury

Web: www.home.att.net/~selectfest/
E-mail: selectfest@worldnet.att.net
Phone: 973-539-4781

Team One
PO Box 8943
Cincinnati, OH 45208
Director: Jeff Spelman

Web: www.teamonebaseball.rivals.com
E-mail: TeamOneBB@aol.com

United States Specialty Sports Association
PO Box 1145
Liberty, MD 64069
Director: Chet Kapla

Web: www.usssa.com
E-mail: rick@KCSports.org
Fax: 816-415-2273
Phone: 816-415-2255

U.S. Tournament of Champions
2613 East Third Street
Bloomington, IN 47401
Director: Carl Lamb

Web: www.ustoc.com
E-mail: infor@ustoc.com
Fax: 812-332-4415
Phone: 812-334-0862 / 332-1420

If you know of a showcase not listed here, please let us know so we can add it in our next edition.

Pro Tryouts
If you get the opportunity to attend an open or invitation-only pro tryout, you should definitely go. The chance to make a positive impression on a pro scout can pay huge dividends for you. College coaches often ask scouts to recommend good high school players who are not ready for pro ball. Check with the Major League Scouting

Bureau (909-980-1881) for a list of pro tryouts in your area.

PRODUCING A HIGHLIGHT VIDEO

A highlight video allows coaches who do not get an opportunity to see you in person evaluate your skills accurately. By watching your tape, coaches can personally decide if you're a prospective recruit by assessing your speed, arm strength, hitting, and fielding abilities. He doesn't have to rely on someone else's evaluation that may be biased.

Coaches are not critiquing your video editing skills; so don't worry about making yours look like a segment on ESPN. If you are concerned about producing your own video, you can hire professionals, who will do everything for you. If you choose to save the money (some companies will charge you $500 or more!) and do it yourself, follow these steps:

1. Shoot the footage in a practice setting. Don no attempt to get game footage - it's too difficult to get useful shots. Use your local field, gym (if it's too cold) or a batting cage. If you already have good game clips, you can include them. This usually works best for pitchers.
2. Wear a full uniform so you look like a ballplayer.
3. Get right to the action! Edit out all dead time periods where there is no action (i.e. the five seconds you take adjusting your batting gloves and getting ready in between cuts).
4. Limit the length of the tape to four minutes. Coaches will not watch long videos. Less is better.
5. Use a tripod at all times so the camera doesn't shake.
6. Tell the cameraman or anyone within earshot to avoid "cheerleading" by saying things like, "Great hit!" or "Cannon arm!" The only sound should come from the action on the field.
7. Make sure to shoot from angles that coaches want to see (use diagrams that follow).
8. If you have access to video-editing software, you can shoot all the footage and edit it at home on your computer. If you don't, you will need to record over clips you do not want to include. The tape should only feature your best performances.
9. Convert the finished tape to VHS format and make as many copies as you need. Use a sticker to label the tape with your name, graduation year, position, address, and phone number. Make sure to write the title - i.e. "Jeff Wilson's 4-minute highlight tape ('06 Grad)"

Introduction
Place the camera on a tripod a few feet away and introduce yourself. Speak clearly and confidently. Practice so it sounds conversational and not like you're reading a cue card. Include:
- Full name and graduation year
- High school's name and your coach's name
- City and state where you live
- Height & weight
- Position(s)
- SAT/ACT scores and GPA
- What you want to study in college (if you're undecided, it's okay to say you're undecided, but just mention some of your interests at this point like liberal arts or business)

Make sure you put all of your contact information - your full name, position, address, phone number - on a sticker on the outside of your videotape (both on top and on the spine). It's very possible that this tape might get separated from the rest of your materials in a college coach's office, and you don't want the coach to get you mixed up with another recruit. Remember, the easier you make it for the coaches, the more open they will be to you.

Copyright 2008 Mazz Marketing   203--260-4932   Wayne@WayneMazzoni.com

Pitchers

Shots 1-12: Place the camera half way between home plate and the mound. It should be slightly toward 3B if you're a righty, or slightly toward first base if you're a lefty. Avoid filming from behind the catcher or backstop; it's too far away. The coach wants to evaluate your mechanics. If you have a radar gun, place it behind the catcher (RG) and cut to a quick clip of it one time for each type of pitch you throw.

Shots 13-21: Place the camera behind the pitcher and capture the flight of the ball to the catcher. It should be positioned slightly toward SS if you're a righty, or slightly toward 2B's position if you're a lefty.

SHOT	PITCH TYPE	SITUATION	CAMERA POSITION
1-5	Fastball	Wind-up	R1 or L1
6	Fastball	Stretch	R1 or L1
7	Change-up	Wind-up	R1 or L1
8	Change-up	Stretch	R1 or L1
9	Curve	Wind-up	R1 or L1
10	Curve	Stretch	R1 or L1
11	Any other	Wind-up	R1 or L1
12	Any other	Stretch	R1 or L1
13	Fastball	Wind-up	R2 or L2
14	Fastball	Wind-up	R2 or L2
15	Fastball	Stretch	R2 or L2
16	Change-up	Wind-up	R2 or L2
17	Change-up	Stretch	R2 or L2
18	Curve	Wind-up	R2 or L2
19	Curve	Stretch	R2 or L2
20	Any other	Wind-up	R2 or L2
21	Any other	Stretch	R2 or L2

Outfielders -- Stand in right field, about 260 feet from the plate.

Shots 1-4: Place the camera at the 2B's position. The cameraman should get a close up of you so the coach can evaluate your footwork, positioning, and mechanics. Keep the camera focused on you - do not let the cameraman follow the flight of the ball. Make sure to throw a line-drive, one hopper to 3B.

Shots 5-10: Place the camera behind the third base line and then behind the catcher so the coach can evaluate the flight of the ball.

SHOT	FUNGO TYPE	THROW TO	CAMERA POSITION
1	Pop Fly	3B	CP1
2	Ground Ball	3B	CP1
3	Pop Fly	Home	CP1
4	Ground Ball	Home	CP1
5	Pop Fly	3B	CP2
6	Ground Ball	3B	CP2
7	Ground Ball	3B	CP2
8	Pop Fly	Home	CP3
9	Ground Ball	Home	CP3
10	Ground Ball	Home	CP3

If you have a radar gun, place it behind 1B (RG) and cut to a quick clip of the reading one time.

Middle Infielders & Third Basemen -- Stand at deep SS

Shots 1-6: Place the camera between the mound and home plate. Have the cameraman focus on you and capture all your movements in the frame and the last 15 feet or so of the ball before it reaches you. The coach wants to evaluate your hands, footwork, the way you circle the ball, and your throwing mechanics.

Shots 7-12: Place the camera behind 1B so the coach can see the flight of the ball.

SHOT	FUNGO TYPE	THROW TO	CAMERA POSITION
1-2	Grounder directly at you	1B	CP1
3	Grounder to your left	1B	CP1
4	Grounder to your right	1B	CP1
5	Slow grounder to charge	1B	CP1
6	Grounder directly at you	2B	CP1
7-8	Grounder directly at you	1B	CP2
9	Grounder to your left	1B	CP2
10	Grounder to your right	1B	CP2
11	Slow grounder you charge	1B	CP2
12	Grounder to 2B to you	1B	CP2

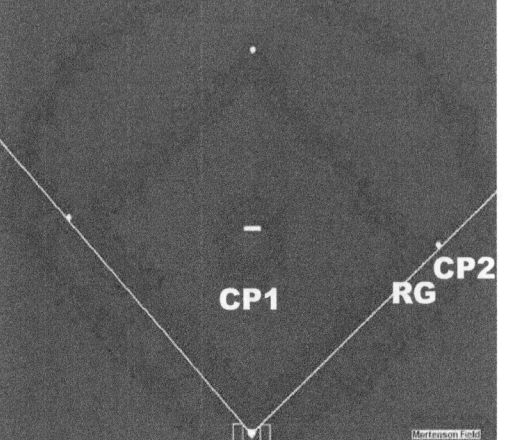

If you have a radar gun, place it behind 1B (RG) and cut to a quick clip of the reading one time.

First Basemen -- Stand at deep 1B so you'll have a long throw across the diamond.

Shots 1-5: Place the camera between the mound and home plate. Have the cameraman focus on you and capture all your movements in the frame and the last 15 feet or so of the ball before it reaches you. The coach wants to evaluate your hands, footwork, and your throwing mechanics.

Shots 6-10: Place the camera behind 3B. Have the cameraman focus on yu and the flight of the ball. The coach wants to evaluate your footwork, arm strength, and throwing accuracy.

SHOT	FUNGO TYPE	THROW TO	CAMERA POSITION
1	Grounder directly at you	3B	CP1
2	Grounder directly at you	3B	CP1
3	Grounder to your left	3B	CP1
4	Grounder to your right	3B	CP1
5	Slow grounder that you charge	3B	CP1
6	Grounder directly at you	3B	CP2
7	Grounder directly at you	3B	CP2
8	Grounder to your left	3B	CP2
9	Grounder to your right	3B	CP2
10	Slow grounder that you charge	3B	CP2

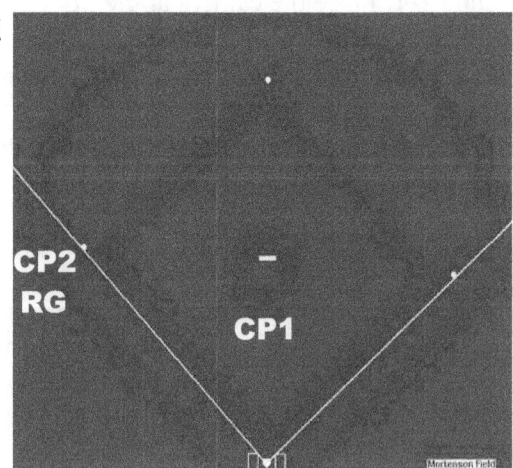

If you have a radar gun, place it behind 3B (RG) and cut to a quick clip of the reading one time.

Catchers -- Get in your crouch behind the plate and wear your full equipment. Have the pitcher stand about 40 feet away and throw batting practice speed pitches to you. You will need a stopwatch to record your pop to pop time (the time it takes from the instant the ball hits your glove until it hits the 2B's glove).

Shots 1-9: Place the camera between home plate and the mound so the coach can see how you block the ball, frame the ball, your footwork, quickness, and your throwing mechanics.

Shots 10-11: Place the camera behind 2B so the coach can evaluate the flight of your throw during a steal situation.

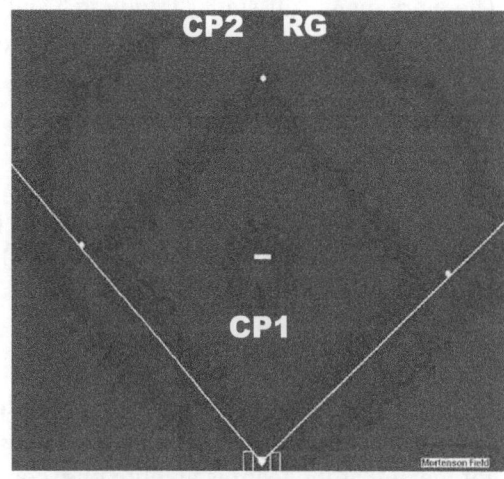

SHOT	TYPE OF PITCH	THROW TO	CAMERA POSITION
1	Right to your glove	2B	CP1
2	Right to your glove	2B	CP1
3-4	In the dirt directly at you	None	CP1
5-6	In the dirt to your right	None	CP1
7-8	In the dirt to your left	None	CP1
9	Slow bunt	2B	CP1
10-11	Right to your glove	2B	CP2

If you have a radar gun, place it behind 2B (RG) and cut to a quick clip of the reading one time. Cut to a quick clip of the stopwatch after shots 1 and 2.

Hitting

Place the camera about 10 feet away so your whole body fills the screen. If you're a righty, place the camera near the 1B batting circle. If you're a lefty, place the camera near the 3B batting circle. The coach is evaluating your stance, bat speed, balance, and swing mechanics. Take about 15 swings.

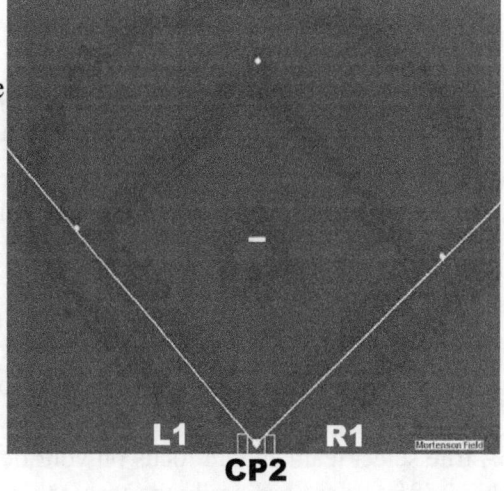

SHOT	TYPE OF PITCH	HIT	CAMERA POSITION
1	Slow BP speed	Bunt	R1 or L1
2-11	Slow BP speed	Hit-away	R1 or L1
12-21	Slow BP speed	Hit-away	CP2

If you are primarily a pitcher, you do not need to video your hitting on the tape unless your skills are exceptional

Running

Every coach will want to evaluate your foot speed and quickness. You will need a stopwatch. Place the camera about 10 feet behind the finish line. If you are a catcher, pitcher, or a below average runner for your position, you should not include running on your video.

Shot 1: Home to 1B. Get in your batting stance and have someone throw a slow pitch to you. Swing as if it were a game situation, drop the bat, and sprint down the line. Start the stopwatch the moment contact is made with the ball and stop it when you touch 1B. Just run one time and cut to a quick clip of the reading on the stopwatch. Place the camera behind 1B.

Shot 2: 60-yard dash. If you don't have a tape measure to mark off 60 yards, use your school's football field. Just run one time and cut to a quick clip of the reading on the stop watch. Place the camera behind the finish line.

TRAVEL, ALL-STAR & SELECT TEAMS

Research needs to be done to determine which travel, all-star, or select teams to try out for to gain the maximum quality of experience and exposure, and which college camps, and which showcase camps are truly valuable to attract the right college coaches' attention.

There are many "all-star," "traveling," and "select" teams, for instance, but many of these teams don't attract coaches to their games. The same holds true for showcase camps. Some of these camps may be expensive, but don't really provide an effective showcase for the player. It's imperative to do your research before you invest your time and money.

All teams are not created equal. In recent years, their numbers have grown enormously, diluting the talent base. Just about anyone can create such a team. It pays to do some research to determine if a particular team is truly made up of above-average players and if they compete against the kind of competition that a college coach views as superior.

One test to see if the team you're considering is a true select team is to gauge the competition they play against. If it's mostly local and their schedule is fairly indiscriminate, chances are they're not a bona fide select team. Some parents may pick teams that are "select" in their eyes only. Also, just because a team "travels" does not mean that the team is an elite one, composed of superior players. A true select team is composed of the caliber of players and plays the level of competition that regularly attracts college (and pro) coaches and scouts to their contests.

If college coaches don't normally attend at least a few of their games to see the players on that team, it may not be the best team to get noticed on. It doesn't really count if the coach of such a team claims that there have been scouts at their games in the past, if the only reason the college coaches and scouts were there was because they happened to be playing a team that was regularly scouted. That would be relying on lightning to strike and the odds aren't in your favor if you hope to get noticed by accident on such a team.

What Is Their Focus?
Is it primarily to prepare players (the younger aged teams) for high school ball? If so, that might not give you the exposure you're looking for. A true select team very likely takes the assumption, based on the quality of players selected, that your high school tryout will most likely be the easiest tryout you'll have.

A true select team should focus on your development as a college and/or pro player. Teams that truly have that kind of focus are ordinarily the teams that college coaches are interested in watching as they know the talent level on the team is more likely going to be what they're after.

How Many Games Do They Play?
If they play relatively few games, especially in a cold climate, then they probably aren't a bona fide select team. If you live in Indiana, for example, and the team you're considering only plays 40-50 games in a season, that's probably not a true select team. You'll play more than that in a Rec league, but not nearly enough to gain the kind of playing experience a player from say Florida or Texas will have, who will play at least twice as many games.

Who Do They Play?
Is their competition high-level competition or are you aware of other teams that play much tougher teams regularly?

Who Coaches The Team?
Is it the father of one of the players? Many of the best select teams don't allow parents to coach their own offspring (for obvious reasons). Also, is the coach paid or does he or she work on a volunteer basis? Many of the best select teams pay their coaches. Also, what are the coach's qualifications? Did he or she play college or professional baseball?

What's The Team Practice-To-Games Ratio?
If it's all games and only a few or no practices, it may still be a good quality team, but many times teams that don't practice much don't really teach the players much, either. At higher ages, practices may be fewer as most players will also participate on the high school level during that season and the summer teams take that into consideration. At younger levels, however, the practice-to-games ratio is more important.

How Many Players Make The Team?
If the number is so large that it's obvious several players aren't going to get much playing time, then that team might not be a good fit. A baseball team carrying say 16 players means that at least 3-4 of those players probably will log a lot of pine time. It's more important to play a lot for a lesser team than sit on the bench for a more prestigious team.

What If I Can't Make A Select or Travel Team or Can't Afford One?
Don't worry about it! It does help for most players, simply because as a rule you'll compete against better competition, have better coaching and get much more experience, but sometimes it's just not practical or possible to be on such a team. If, for any reason, you can't get on a select team, then make up for it in other ways -- more practice individually, private coaching, etc.

BOTTOM OF THE NINTH
This was a long and information-packed chapter, and one that you'll no doubt want to refer back to on many occasions.

Now that you have all this information about how to take an active role in your recruitment, it's time to get started. Here's a quick checklist of things you can begin doing:
- Prepare your written profile.
- Send out Letters of Interest to the schools on your Target List.
- Develop a web page for yourself.
- Plan and take campus visits.
- Produce a highlight video.
- Contact some showcases and make plans to attend.
- Research local select teams you would be interested in playing for.

6
DRIVE DOWN THE COST OF COLLEGE

In This Chapter

- Where to find scholarship money other than for baseball
- How to determine how much money you need and your "family contribution"
- The various types of financial aid and when forms should be submitted
- Tips for receiving a good aid package and where to find loans

This chapter may have you scratching your head. After all, if a goal of this guide is to help you get a baseball scholarship, why do you need to worry about paying for college? Well, as we've said before, athletic scholarships are difficult to obtain and most don't cover all of your costs. Even if you're the next Roger Clemens, the chances are good you're going to have to pay for at least some of your college expenses and possibly locate any scholarship or financial aid dollars to assist you and your parents with the upcoming costs.

FACTS ABOUT FINANCIAL AID

Baseball Scholarships
Baseball scholarships are extremely rare. Even if you are fortunate enough to receive a partial scholarship, the majority of all scholarship funding is awarded to pitchers. What's left over is usually given to "up the middle" players - catchers, middle infielders, and center fielders. The true "full-ride" scholarships are next to impossible to obtain, so you also should explore non-athletic aid opportunities.

Once again, we remind you that being realistic about the financial aspect of college is just as important as setting your admissions and athletic expectations. Next to purchasing a home, paying for college is the biggest investment you or your parents will likely face. Everyone in the family needs to be on the same page when anticipating expenses and how to reduce them.

 If you would like to compare the costs of your Target Schools, use our worksheet, "College Cost Comparisons," in Chapter 8.

Financial Aid Helps Roughly 75% of All Students Afford College
Simply put, as much as sports and academic concerns should dictate your Target List schools, the price of college may ultimately have even more to do with where you receive your higher education. The cost of college is high and probably rising - tuition for four years averages $99,784 at a private college or $45,352 at a public university - you should definitely consider applying for financial aid to help pay your college expenses.

Overall college costs can, and should be, an important consideration in your final selection process. With a little research and dedication, however, you can avoid having the expense of college dictate which schools you apply to and attend. There are many ways to alleviate the financial burden, and you must employ a creative plan and investigate all areas of help.

Become familiar with all the sources of aid that are available to you, and constantly stay abreast of this ever-changing landscape. This chapter includes tips on scholarships and financial aid, but we urge you to speak with your guidance counselor and research on your own at web sites like www.collegeanswer.com, www.collegeboard.com, www.scholarships.com, and www.fastweb.com

Another extremely valuable resource comes free with this guide. Now available is a free monthly web seminar giving you all the basics on financial aid. This seminar, from The Institute for College Aid Planning, will give you information on academic and athletic scholarships, loans, grants, and strategies that can be used right now to make the cost of your education more affordable. To access this great information, e-mail Thomas Perrone at The Institute For College Aid Planning at tpicap@comcast.net. Be sure to mention "My Sports Dreams."

Over 600,000 Scholarship Opportunities Available!
www.fastweb.com, an internet scholarship search site, features information on over 600,000 different scholarships and aid programs. Even though it takes a lot of time and paperwork to win this "free" money, it could save your family a lot of money. That makes it well worth the effort. We've already explained how tough it is to get a baseball scholarship, and when you consider that NCAA D-I Ivy and Patriot League Schools (other than American U., recently admitted to the Patriot League), all NCAA D-III schools, and all NJCAA D-III schools do not even offer athletic scholarships, you'll understand how important it can be to locate other aid.

Determine How Much Money You Need
Get out the notebook and calculator. On the next page is a list of general expense categories, which are part of

any college student's budget. To give you and your parents a general idea of how much money it will take to get you through college and launched into adulthood, do some research to come up with approximate figures for each of these categories. Add it all up, and you've got yourself a budget, which needs to be funded from one or more of the following: your parents, your savings and any scholarships or aid programs available to you.

Budget Categories for Your College Education:

- Tuition & Fees
- Room & Board
- Books & Classroom Supplies
- Personal Expenses
- Transportation

A number of sites, such as the ones mentioned above, have a variety of guides and calculators, which let you plug in schools and numbers to come up with anticipated costs for your education.

Family Contribution

Most colleges will expect you and your parents to contribute to your college expenses based upon your parents' annual income and their assets. When referring to the Family Contribution Schedule (see Chapter 8), you will need to know your parents' net assets and annual income before taxes. Take the net assets and read down according to your family size until you get to your parent's annual income, and this will determine your family contribution. Subtract your family contribution from the college cost and the result will indicate the amount of aid that can be available.

Example: If your parents' net assets are $40,000 and their annual income is $44,000 for a family of three, then your family contribution will be $6,869. If the college cost is $15,000, then your aid eligibility would be $8,131.

Loans, Grants, Merit Scholarships, and Work-Study

So, where does the money come from to send you to school? It can come in the form of loans, grants, scholarships, and federal work-study grants. Need-based loans are granted through Perkins or Stafford loan programs. The federal government may also distribute loans to families who have trouble meeting their family contribution. Congress has two programs to assist families in this situation; they are the Parent Loans for Undergraduate Students (PLUS) and the Supplemental Loans for Students (SLS). More than 60% of all financial aid comes in the form of student loans.

You should be careful that your on-campus job is not so time-consuming that it detracts from your studies. Also, be aware that if you make the baseball team, your athletic obligation will require a considerable amount of your free time.

Many need-based financial aid packages may include grants or scholarships. In addition, the college you attend may reward you with a special grant or scholarship for distinguished achievements within a particular area, such as academics or athletics.

The federal work-study program is designed to provide students with on-campus jobs. The jobs range from giving campus tours to filing books in the library. The money you earn in work-study is paid directly to you on a weekly or monthly basis depending upon the school. It can be used to help pay tuition, room and board, books, or any personal expenses.

Financial Aid Forms

To apply for financial aid, you and your parents will have to complete the Free Application for Federal Student Aid (FAFSA). The form can be downloaded from www.fafsa.ed.gov/or you can get it from you local high school guidance counselor. It compiles all your family's finances and rates the information to determine your eligibility for aid. Other forms may include the FAF (Financial Aid Form), the SAAC (Student Aid Application for California), and the FFS (Family Financial Statement).

College Scholarship Service/Financial Aid Profile

Some colleges that offer institutional financial aid ask applicants to complete a "profile" in addition to the FAFSA. The profile requests much more comprehensive and detailed financial information. If asked to submit this form, you should do it, because it could lead to additional money for you. Call 800-778-6888 to register and an application packet will be mailed to you. The application costs $6 to process and $16 for each report they send to schools and organizations.

Timeline

Financial aid forms should be completed and submitted no later than February of your senior year so that you are eligible for assistance. By mid-April, you will receive an award letter from each school where you have been accepted. The packages will vary at each school and may include federal and state grants, school scholarships, student loans, and on-campus jobs. This will allow you to determine which school is offering you the best package.

The Relationship Between The Financial Aid and Admission Offices

Most schools claim that their admissions office and financial aid office are independent and do not influence each other's decisions. Usually, the best overall students are admitted regardless of their financial need, and the average students are evaluated based on how much money they will cost the school.

WHAT YOU NEED TO KNOW ABOUT LOANS

Student loans can be instrumental in making college education affordable, but remember all loans must be paid back. Usually you do not have to start paying on your loans until you either graduate or leave college for an extended period of time. Before taking out a loan, make sure that you and your family understands the exact conditions.

Subsidized Loans
The federal government pays or "subsidizes" the interest on your loans while in college. This reduces the amount of money you have to pay back over the life of your loan. A subsidized loan is awarded on the basis of financial need.

Grace Period
All student loans have a six to nine month grace period between the time you leave college and the time you start paying back your loans. Even if you do not graduate from college, you will still be expected to repay your loans. The repayment period for parent loans begins shortly after the loan is disbursed.

Loan Deferment
If you have an emergency that prevents you from repaying your loan, you can request a temporary loan deferment so that you do not have to pay your loans during this time. You must apply and be approved before you can qualify for a loan deferment.

Promissory Note
When applying for a student loan you must sign a legal document where you "promise" to repay the loan plus the accrued interest.

Default
If you do not repay the loan according to the terms of the promissory note, you are in default, and your credit rating and eligibility for future financial aid will be jeopardized.

For more information on loans check out these websites:

Chela Financial	www.loans4students.org
Nel Net	www.nelnet.net
FinAid	www.finaid.org
Students.gov	www.students.gov

TERMS

FAFSA - (free Application for Federal Student Aid) Form you must complete in order to determine your eligibility to receive financial aid from any college in the U.S.

EFC - (Estimated Family Contribution) Based on the information on your FAFSA, this is the government's calculation of the amount your family can afford to contribute towards college expenses. Indicates financial need.

SAR - (Student Aid Report) includes your EFC and is sent to the colleges you listed on your FAFSA.

TAP - (Tuition Assistance Program) Provides New York State students, who demonstrate financial need, with grants that range from $100 - $5000. Only New York State students who plan to attend college I New York are eligible.

HEOP/EOP - (Higher/Education Opportunity Program) Available at some public and private colleges in New York State. Provides financial and academic support for students who are educationally and economically disadvantaged.

FSEOG - (Federal Supplemental Educational Opportunity Grant) Awarded to students who demonstrate exceptional need. Limited and only distributed by some colleges. Grants range from $100 - $4000 per year.

Pell Grants - Federal grants that range from $400 - $4000 per academic year and are awarded to students who demonstrate financial need.

FWS - (Federal Work Study) Awards college jobs to students to earn money to pay various school-related expenses.

CSS Profile - College Scholarship Search Profile) Financial aid form required by many private colleges. There are registration and other fees associated with this form.

APTS - (Aid for Part-Time Study) Awarded to part-time students who live and attend colleges in new York State. APTS provides grants of up to $200 per academic year.

TIPS FOR RECEIVING THE BEST PACKAGE

Apply to Expensive Schools, Even If You Need a Lot Of Aid
If an expensive college sees you as a desirable candidate, you should definitely apply, regardless of your financial situation. As long as you have a financial need, the school will provide the money you need. Believe it or not, you could actually pay less to attend a high-tuition private school than a lower cost state school. Knowing that your family contribution can be roughly the same at schools with varying costs will enable you to concentrate on non-financial considerations in selecting schools to apply to.

If your parents' income is too high and you do not qualify for need-based aid, you may find that merit aid puts a high-sticker school within reach. Colleges are awarding more merit aid packages in order to attract higher-caliber students. Most colleges are able to meet the financial needs of all of their students, but keep in mind that a lot of packages feature mostly federal loans and work-study and fewer grants. And that means you will be paying off these loans for years to come.

Negotiate a Better Deal At Your First-Choice School By Playing Colleges Against Each Other
Most aid administrators agree that if you don't get the aid you think you need, you should appeal your case. Your circumstances may warrant a second look, or a mistake on your applications could come to light. Frequent mistakes include claiming college expenses for a sibling who has dropped out and stating your adjusted gross income instead of the total.

If you want to try to increase your financial aid package, make sure you do it in a tactful way. Ask the financial aid officer if you can "appeal" your offer. Don't use the term "negotiate," because it has a negative connotation. Explain that you really want to go to the school and you would really appreciate it if the school would consider adjusting your package.

Be honest and provide copies of the other offers you have received. Explain how much of an increase you need before you can enroll. You have nothing to lose by asking. Even though most financial aid officers do not want to get dragged into a bidding war, you should still request a better package with your first choice school. If you're a highly sought-after prospect, they will make every effort to meet your request.

Ask your guidance counselor to call the financial aid department and request the adjustment on your behalf. Most students who take this route find that their package increases. Also, if you win an outside scholarship, make sure to get the scholarship provider involved. Big companies who provide scholarships have a lot of clout with financial aid officers. If a school upsets a parent or student with its policy, it's just one student and one tuition at stake. But the school risks a wealth of future funding when they displease a prominent scholarship provider.

Watch Out For Scam Artists!
Watch out for "financial aid advisors" who offer their services for a fee and do any of the following things:
- Promise you a scholarship. (No one can guarantee you an award.)
- Say the "scholarships" they will help you find are not publicized. Scholarships widely publicize their competitions because they want to choose the winner from a strong pool of applicants.)
- Offer to search a scholarship database for you. (Never pay for this service -

it's free!)
- Pressure you to commit right away. (Avoid fast-talking salesmen.)
- Ask inappropriate questions about your finances or related information. This is none of their business.)
- Request your bank or credit card account number to "hold" a scholarship for you. (Never provide this information.)
- Invite you to a free financial planning "seminar." When families arrive, they're hit with a high-pressure sales pitch for costly services that may include career counseling, rearranging assets to increase a family's calculated need for aid, and an "exclusive" scholarship search that, in reality, you could perform at little or no cost. (The services can run as much as $1,000 and offer little or nothing of worth- sometimes a basic skills assessment, perhaps, or canned financial advice.)
- Be sure to check out "Scholarship Scams" at www.ftc.gov

Tips for Getting the Most Aid

- Alert the aid office before you apply to irregularities regarding your parents' finances like an upcoming one-time bonus, pending hospital bills because of a serious illness, an inheritance, a business start-up or serious reversal. The more the office knows, the better.
- Beat the deadline and submit your application before it is due. Dealing with a family's tangled finances during crunch time puts tremendous pressure on over-worked aid representatives. That's when mistakes happen. Also, a lot of aid is awarded on a first-come, first-served basis.
- Get organized. Keep your files updated, know the facts, and maintain a call log to verify whom you've been talking with, when you talked to them, and the content of those conversations.
- Go to the top. If you're not satisfied with what you're hearing from an aid representative, ask politely but firmly to speak with the director of financial aid. Most directors say their phone lines are open to anyone who calls.
- Always answer financial aid applications honestly. If an aid officer ever notices a discrepancy between what you write on your application and your parents' tax returns, you will need to repay the money owed plus fines.

Financial Aid Horror Stories

Samantha - Los Angeles, CA
Samantha from Los Angeles worrying about paying for college landed a dream opportunity. She landed a role in a commercial and figured she could use the $8,000 paycheck to help with college. However, the college added the one time income to her assets and she lost over $3,200 in grant money because of it. She had to increase her student loans and go into debt. To avoid this happening to you keep focused on your grades to help with financial aid and be careful how much you work. A key fact to know is the federal government reduces aid by 50 cents for every dollar over $2,500 you earn. Even worse, they reduce aid by 85 cents for every dollar over $2,500 you have saved.

Louisa - Dallas, TX
Another example shows the importance of the deadline. When Louisa's family received financial aid forms in January they did not have all of the information they needed to fill them out (tax returns). Her father waited until March when he received the information and immediately sent out the forms. However, when Louisa received her aid award letter it was $10,000 less than then prior year. By the time the office received her forms all of the grant

money was gone. Some tips to avoid this happening to you:
1. Take deadlines seriously
2. Send all forms in as soon as possible, there is no harm in them being early
3. If you do not yet have your tax return there is a form FAFSA uses to estimate it until you receive it.

Legitimate Ways to Help Increase Your Aid Package

- Use savings to pay off credit cards, car loans, or other debt. These items are not figured into your family's net assets. The lower your family's assets and income, the more aid you will receive.
- Avoid taking large capital gains in the year used to determine aid. These gains count as both assets and income.
- Reduce assets in the student's name. Federal law requires that 35% of those assets must be defined as the student's share of first-year expenses, while the take is no more than about 5.6% of parents' assets (and roughly $40,000 is not counted).
- Notify the financial aid office in writing about anything unusual in your family's financial situation like a large medical expense.

Apply For Local Scholarships

Many corporations and non-profit organizations offer scholarship competitions. Your high school's guidance office probably keeps a list of scholarships, and it's smart to call organizations to see if they offer awards. Churches, Synagogues, 4-H Clubs, Rotary Clubs, Kiwanis Clubs, Lions Club, and Boys & Girls Clubs are all good places to start. The Internet site www.FastWeb.com is also a great resource. Some of these scholarships may only amount to a few hundred dollars, but every little bit helps!

Write the Best Application Essays You Can

It will be well worth the effort. Ask your parents and teachers to critique your drafts. You can reuse the same essay for different applications, but make sure to personalize it for the specific award. Some important tips to write good essays:
- Be yourself
- Don't be gimmicky
- Think small (Most college application essays are 500 words which is not enough for a complex story).
- Don't wait until the last minute
- Don't let someone else write your essay (You could get caught and admissions counselors generally know how 17 and 18 year olds write)
- Revise
- Proofread more than once

Low-Interest Rates on College Loans Available

If your family is like most others in the United States and is unable to completely afford college expenses, you can take out a low-interest loan. (The rates have fallen at the time of publication to their lowest levels in years.) Remember, you don't need to borrow the amount needed for all four years. You just need enough to get you through one year at a time.

Tuition Payment Plans

For roughly $50 per year, Academic Management Services (508-235-2900), a financial service company can spread your tuition payments over 10 to 12 months, interest-free. This way you don't have to pay the entire first year bill in one lump sum. Many universities also offer an interest-free monthly payment plan, managed either by a company like Academic Management Services or by the school itself.

Free Aid Information Available On-Line
Two of the best Web sites, say financial-aid experts, are FastWEB (www.fastweb.com/) and US News & World Reports (www.usnews.com/). Both feature comprehensive searchable databases of scholarships, so you can enter information such as age, gender, class rank, and track of study and pull up a list of grants and loans that fit your profile.

Be Careful About How Much Money You Borrow
Last year, more than five million students borrowed a record $40 billion for college, three times the 1990 level. At some schools, graduates leave campus with an average debt of $30,000. To make matters worse, most undergraduates misjudge how much they're going to owe after they leave college, and how this debt might affect their future plans.

To avoid any surprises, visit an aid officer periodically during college, beginning in January of your freshman year, keep track of how fast the loans are piling up and get some help on how to build your loan repayment obligations into compensation you will receive when you enter the work force. One way to stay abreast of your accumulating federal debt is by visiting the National Student Loan Data System (www.nslds.ed.gov/which provides personalized information online.

Sample Scholarships You Can Win!
There are over 4,000 scholarship opportunities for you. Go to www.FreeScholarshipGuide.com for a complete list. Here is a small sample:

Scholarship	Value	Link
AICPA Scholarships	Up to $5,000	www.aicpa.org
Barry M. Goldwater Scholarship	Up to $7,500	www.act.org/goldwater
Burger King Scholars Program	$1,000	www.bkscholars.csfa.org
Collegenet Scholarship	Up to $10,000	www.collegenet.com
Elks National Foundation	$1,000 to $15,000 per year	www.elks.org/enf/scholars
Japanese American Citizens League	30 scholarships from $1,000-$5,000	www.jacl.org
John F. Kennedy "Profile in Courage" Essay Contest	$500-$3,000	www.jfkcontest.org
got milk? SAMMY Awards	25 scholarships of $7,500	www.whymilk.com/index.htm
MBNA Foundation Award	$1,000 to $7,500 (renewable)	www.mbnafoundation.org
The Ron Brown Scholar Program	$40,000	www.ronbrown.org
Robert C. Byrd Honors Scholarship	$4,000 to $6,000	www.ed.gov
Tylenol Scholarship	10 $10,000 awards, 150 $1,000 awards	www.scholarship.tylenol.com
U.S. Bank's Internet Scholarship Program	Up to 30 $1,000 scholarships	www.usbank.com/studentloans

10 Tips from a Scholarship Judge

1) Use the scholarship application itself- don't type the question over. One applicant thought she was being thorough by typing out each question on another sheet, with her answer underneath it. But, judges go through a lot of applications, and they get used to seeing information in the same place. A typed-out application is harder to read. Plus, this particular applicant left off one of the questions, and knocked her out of the running.
2) Fill out the practice application first. Photocopy the application and use the copy to write a draft. Once you've fine-tuned your answers, type them neatly on the original.
3) Pay attention to detail. Most applications ask for your name, address, date of birth, and expected graduation date. Be careful- omitting information can cost you. The applications I read asked students under 18 to have a parent or guardian sign the form. Applicants who ignored that had a mark against them from the start.
4) Be concise, but creative. What you write- not how much you write will impress Judges. Try to emphasize what makes you different from everybody else. Let your personality show through so judges can feel connected to you.
5) Have some self-respect. When explaining how you overcame hardship, do not milk your difficulties. The judge should admire you and you achievements, not squirm in their seat.
6) Be humble. When reporting accomplishments, be humble. Try to convey your dedication and skill, but also maintain modesty. Watch for a bragging tone.
7) Do the math. If an application asks for your family's income or college expenses, make sure those financial numbers are correct.
8) Choose your teachers wisely. Often, it's hard to pick scholarship winners from a pool of so many excellent entries. Outstanding teacher letters may make the difference.
9) Help your teachers write the best letters. Give them a summary of your achievements and goals and all the scholarship information.
10) Do not miss the deadline. After you work hard putting together the best possible application, make sure it will be read!

BOTTOM OF THE NINTH

Sadly, there are a lot of families who mistakenly believe that their child's tuition will be fully paid-for when they receive an athletic scholarship. Too often, these families get a rude awakening when their child either doesn't get a full ride, or doesn't get a scholarship at all.

Now's the time to take an honest look at your family's financial situation and begin to look at your options for paying for college. Here are some steps to follow:
- Use FastWeb or another service to identify some scholarships you might qualify for.
- Contact local companies/organizations and your school's guidance department to identify local scholarship opportunities.
- Apply for as many scholarships as you can.
- Look into loans and other means of getting aid.
- Work on your application essays.

FINANCIAL AID TIMELINE

November:

- If you are applying for early decision, remember that most schools have deadlines in mid-November.
- Check if your high school offers any free workshops on how to complete financial aid forms.

December:

- Complete your FAFSA, but do not mail it until January 1st. Make sure you have properly signed and dated the document. Any mistakes can delay the process and result in lost financial aid.
- Keep copies of everything you mail.

January:

- To qualify for the most aid possible, submit your FAFSA as early as you can after January 1st.
- If you sent your FAFSA on January 1st or shortly after that, you should receive a Student Aid Report (SAR) indicating your eligibility for aid and your family's expected contribution.
- Make any corrections to your SAR, including updates based on your family's federal 1040 tax form
- Sign, date, and return the SAR to the address designated.

March:

- Receive a corrected SAR if needed
- Make sure a copy of the corrected SAR reaches the financial aid office at each college you are applying to.

April:

- You may receive notices of admission and financial aid awards. You can begin to compare offers.

May:

- May 1 is the traditional Candidate's Reply Date. You must accept an offer from one school and decline all others.
- Complete any loan forms.

June & July:

- Consider working during the summer so you will have money for expenses when you arrive on campus.
- Continue to look for scholarships. You will need funds beyond freshman year and new scholarships appear every year. Make note of which of your scholarships are renewable.

SERVE YOUR COUNTRY & GET A GREAT EDUCATION!

Army - U.S. Military Academy, NY

Division - ROTC
What You Get - Full scholarship (tuition, books, fees); stipend up to $400/month while in school
What You Give - 4 years of active duty; 4 years reserve duty; 1 ROTC class per semester; weekly drills
To Qualify - SAT: 920; ACT: 19; Age 17-21
Info - 800-USA-ROTC; goarmy.com

Division - Active GI Bill
What You Get - Up to $32,400 for college after discharge; with Army College Fund up to $50,000 in some military job areas; student loan repayment up to $65,000; 75% tuition assistance during service
What You Give - At least 2 years of active duty, $1,200 contribution over course of one year toward benefit
To Qualify - H.S. diploma or equivalent; Age 17-35
Info - 800-USA-ARMY; goarmy.com

Division - Reserve GI Bill
What You Get - $9,936 for college after discharge; loan repayment up to $20,000
What You Give - 1 weekend/ month; 2 weeks/year for 6 years
To Qualify - H.S. diploma or equivalent; age 17-35
Info - 800-USA-ARMY; goarmy.com

Division - Guard GI Bill
What You Get - Up to $9,936 over 36 months; 75% tuition assistance; all states offer additional tuition assistance programs
What You Give - 3-6 years enlistment; 1 weekend/month; 2 weeks/year
To Qualify - H.S diploma or equivalent
Info - 800-GO-GUARD

NAVY - U.S. Naval Academy, Annapolis, MD

Division - ROTC
What You Get - Full scholarship (tuition, books, fees); stipend up to $400/month while in school
What You Give - 3 years active duty; 5 years reserve duty
To Qualify - SAT: 1050; ACT: 22
Info - 800-NAV-ROTC; https://www.nrotc.navy.mil/

Division - Active GI Bill
What You Get - Up to $28,800; with Navy College Fund up to $15,000 in some jobs; 75% tuition assistance up to $3,500/year; seaman-to-admiral (STA), $10,000; tuition repayment up to $10,000
What You Give - 2-6 years active duty; $1,200 contribution (STA: 5 years active duty upon commissioning)
To Qualify - H.S diploma or equivalent (STA: SAT -1000; ACT-21) Age 18-34
Info - 800-USA-NAVY; navyjobs.com

Division - Reserve GI Bill
What You Get - $9,936 for college after discharge; loan repayment up to $20,000
What You Give - 1 weekend/month; 2 weeks/year; 4-6 years active duty
To Qualify - H.S. diploma or equivalent; Age 21-38
Info - 866-NAVRES1; navalreserve.com

MARINES

Division - ROTC
What You Get - Full scholarship (tuition, books, fees); stipend $200/month while in school
What You Give - 4-6 years active duty
To Qualify - SAT: 1050; ACT: 22
Info - 800-USA-NAVY; https://www.nrotc.navy.mil/

Division - Active GI Bill
What You Get - Up to $28,000 after discharge; 100% tuition assistance
What You Give - 3-5 years active duty; $1,200 contribution
To Qualify - H.S. diploma or equivalent
Info - 800-MARINES; marines.com

Division - Reserve GI Bill
What You Get - $7,124.40 for college after discharge
What You Give - 1 weekend/month; 2 weeks/year for 6 years
To Qualify - H.S. diploma or equivalent
Info - 800-MARINES; marines.com

AIR FORCE - U.S. Air Force Academy, Colorado Springs, CO

Division - ROTC
What You Get - Full scholarship; books up to $510/year; stipend up to $400/month
What You Give - 4 years active duty
To Qualify - SAT: 1100; ACT: 24
Info - 866-4AFROTC; afrotc.com

Division - Active GI Bill
What You Get - Up to $40,000 after discharge; college credit for training; 100% tuition assistance up to $4,500/year; loan repayment up to $10,000
What You Give - 4-6 years active duty; $1,200 contribution plus; $600 to increase benefit by $5,400
To Qualify - H.S. diploma or equivalent
Info - 800-423-USAF; airforce.com

Division - Reserve GI Bill
What You Get - Up to $9,936; more for some jobs; 100% tuition assistance up to $4,500/year during service
What You Give - 1 weekend/month; 2 weeks/year for 6 years
To Qualify - H.S. diploma or equivalent
Info - 800-257-1212; afreserve.com
Division - Selected Reserve Guard GI Bill

What You Get - Up to $9,036; state National Guard units offer additional tuition assistance and loan repayment benefits
What You Give - 3-6 years enlistment; 1 weekend/month; 2 weeks/year
To Qualify - H.S. diploma or equivalent
Info - 800-TO-GO-ANG; af.mil

Coast Guard - U.S. Coast Guard, New London, CT

Division - ROTC - No ROTC; College Student Pre-Commissioning Program for qualifying minority students
What You Get - $1,200/month during last two years
What You Give - 3 years active duty
To Qualify - SAT l: 1000; SAT ll: 1100; ACT: 21; GPA: 2.5
Info - 877-NOW-USCG; gocoastguard.com

Division - Active GI Bill
What You Get - Up to $28,000
What You Give - 4-6 years active duty; 2-4 years reserve duty; $1,200 contribution
To Qualify - H.S. diploma or equivalent
Info - 877-NOW-USCG gocoastguard.com

Division - Reserve GI Bill
What You Get - $9,936 for college after discharge; loan repayment up to $20,000
What You Give - 1 weekend/month; 2 weeks/year for 4 years
To Qualify - H.S. diploma or equivalent
Info - 800-424-8883; uscg.mil

*As of 2005. Contact branch above to confirm all information.

Military Stories

"Through the Guard, I served one weekend a month and trained two weeks a year, and they paid 100 percent of my tuition for my degree in criminal justice. You have to be prepared to serve overseas - I worked with the military police in Uzbekistan. I hope to eventually work for local or state police."
-Jarred Tiberi, Sergeant, Military Police, U.S. ArmyNational Guard, Melrose, MA

"I have been in the Army almost three years, and I have completed about 15 credit hours. I am currently taking two more classes toward my associate degree in criminal justice, and the Army gives 100 percent tuition assistance. One of the best programs is the EARMYU, which allows me to continue college study online."
-Ronzale C. Piersey, Sergeant U.S. Army, Fort Knox, KY

"In high school, I joined Navy ROTC, and after graduation, I joined the Marines. I took a military 'skills' test that told me I was suited for personnel administration, which is what I wanted to do. I plan on getting a degree in business administration taking advantage of tuition assistance.
-Veronica Robledo, Lance Corporal, Personnel Administration, U.S. Marines, Quantico, VA

7
THE COLLEGE LANDSCAPE BY DIVISION

In This Chapter

- NCAA Division I
- NCAA Division II
- NCAA Division III
- NAIA
- NJCAA Division I
- NJCAA Division II
- NJCAA Division III

Now, it's time to get a clear picture of just how many options you truly have. This chapter lists all of the colleges and universities that offer baseball programs and details the eligibility requirements for each of the divisions.

NATIONAL COLLEGIATE ATHLETIC ASSOCIATION (NCAA)

The NCAA is the most powerful governing body for college baseball. It represents three separate divisions (I, II, and III) featuring 777 four-year schools.

Contact Info
NCAA
700 W. Washington St.
P.O. Box 6222
Indianapolis, IN 46206-6222
Web: www.ncaa.org/
Phone: 317-917-6222
Fax: 317-917-6888
Publications: 888-388-9748

NCAA Clearinghouse
P.O. Box 4044
Iowa City, IA 52243-4044
Phone: 319-337-1492 or 888-388-9748
Fax: 319-337-1556
To check the status of your filing: 319-339-3003

NCAA Clearinghouse
You must register with the NCAA Clearinghouse after your junior year if you want to be considered an eligible recruit. This lets colleges know that you have met all their academic requirements.

To register, call 888-388-9748 to receive your free copy of the NCAA Guide for the college-Bound Student Athlete. This guide provides detailed information about the NCAA's requirements and contains a Student Release Form. Mail or fax the white copy of the form to the Clearinghouse with the $30 registration fee. Give the yellow and pink copies of the form to your guidance counselor who will send the yellow copy along with your transcript to the Clearinghouse.

The Clearinghouse will send your eligibility status to any NCAA D-I or D-II school that requests it.

It is also very helpful to keep track of your eligibility yourself. Instead of only relying on your high school guidance counselor, keep track of your own eligibility status by checking that you are taking all of the required classes and are maintaining an acceptable GPA. Many websites will help you do this. One good example is www.Prep48.com, which will prevent you from making a mistake and costing yourself years of eligibility. The website is free so login and track your progress throughout your four years of high school.

NCAA DIVISION I

D-I schools are mostly comprised of big schools that attract considerable media attention. They have the largest baseball budgets and recruit players nationally. They are the most popular with high school students because of their high-profile status. There are 282 D-I schools in the country, and each is permitted to award 11.7 full scholarships. The Ivy League and Patriot League schools do not award scholarships.

Academic Eligibility Requirements - Division I

Depending on your three criteria -- GPA, SAT/ACT exam scores, and core courses -- you will either be classified as a "Qualifier," "Partial Qualifier," or "Non Qualifier." Here are the requirements for each:

Qualifier Requirements

- Graduate High School
- Graduate with a core-course GPA (based on a 4.0 scale) and total SAT/ACT scores based on the Qualifier Index below.
- Successfully complete a core curriculum of at least 13 academic course units as follows:
    - 4 years of English
    - 2 years of Math
    - 2 years of Social Science
    - 2 years of Natural or Physical Science (including one lab class)
    - 1 additional year in English, Math, or Natural or Physical Science.
    - 2 more years of any of the above or Foreign Language, Computer Science, Philosophy, or Non-doctrinal Religion

Qualifier Index

Core GPA	ACT-New	SAT-Old	SAT-New
2.5 & Above	68	700	820
2.475	70	710	830
2.450	70	720	840-850
2.425	70	730	860
2.400	71	740	860
2.375	72	750	870
2.350	73	760	880
2.325	74	770	890
2.300	75	780	900
2.275	76	790	910
2.250	77	800	920
2.225	78	810	930
2.200	79	820	940
2.175	80	830	950
2.150	80	840	960
2.125	81	850	960
2.100	82	860	970
2.075	83	870	980
2.050	84	880	990
2.025	85	890	1000
2.000	86	900	1010

Partial Qualifier Requirements

- Graduate High School
- Graduate with a core-course GPA (based on a 4.0 scale) and total SAT/ACT scores based on the Partial Qualifier Index below
- Successfully complete a core curriculum of at least 13 academic course units (same courses as "Qualifier Requirements")

If you are a Partial Qualifier, you cannot play in games during your first year at a Division I school, but you can practice with the team at the home facility and receive a scholarship. You will have three seasons left of eligibility. You can earn a fourth year of eligibility if you receive a bachelor's degree before the start of your fifth year of college.

Partial Qualifier Index

Core GPA	ACT-New	SAT-Old	SAT-New
2.750 & Above	59	600	720
2.725	59	610	730
2.700	60	620	730
2.2.675	61	630	740-750
2.650	62	640	760
2.625	63	650	770
2.600	64	660	780
2.575	65	670	790
2.550	66	680	800
2.525	67	690	810

Non-Qualifier

You will be classified as a Non-Qualifier if you fail to graduate from high school or do not meet the core-curriculum GPA and SAT/ACT scores required for a Qualifier.

If you are a Non-Qualifier, you cannot practice with the team, play games, or receive a baseball scholarship during your first year. You will have three seasons left of eligibility. You can earn a fourth year of eligibility if you receive a bachelor degree before the start of your fifth year of college.

Division I
2008 and Later
If you enroll in a Division I college in 2008 or later and want to play baseball or receive an athletic scholarship during your first year, you must:
- Graduate from high school;
- Complete these 16 core courses:
  - 4 years of English
  - 3 years of math (algebra 1 or higher)
  - 2 years of natural or physical science (including one year of lab science if offered
  - 1 extra year of English, math or natural or physical science
  - 2 years of social science
  - 4 years of extra core courses (from any category above, foreign language, religion or philosophy)
- Earn a minimum required grade-point average in your core courses; and
- Earn a combined SAT or ACT sum score that matches your core-course grade-point average and test score sliding scale above (for example, a 2.400 core-course grade-point average needs a 860 SAT).

NCAA DIVISION II

D-II schools are medium-sized schools and recruit on a smaller scale and have fewer scholarship opportunities than D-I schools. There are 194 D-II schools and each is permitted to award nine full scholarships per year.

Academic Eligibility Requirements - Division II
Depending on your three criteria - GPA, SAT/ACT exam scores, and core course - you will either be classified as a Qualifier, Partial Qualifier, or Non Qualifier. Here are the requirements for each:

Qualifier Requirements

- Graduate High School
- Graduate with a 2.0 core-course GPA (based on a 4.0 scale)
- Score a combined SAT score of at least 820 or a 68 sum score on the ACT
- Successfully complete a core curriculum of at least 13 academic course units as follows:
    - 3 years of English
    - 2 years of Math
    - 2 years of Social Science
    - 2 years of Natural or Physical Science (including one lab class)
    - 2 additional years of English, Math, or Natural or Physical Science
    - 2 more years of any of the above or Foreign Language, Computer Science, Philosophy, or Religion

Partial Qualifier

- Graduate High School
- Score a combined SAT score on the verbal and math sections of 820 or a 68 sum score on the ACT, or…
- Graduate with a 2.0 core-course GPA (based on a 4.0 scale) and successfully complete a core curriculum of at least 13 academic courses (same as "Qualifier Requirements")

If you are a Partial Qualifier, you cannot play in games during your first year, but you can practice with the team at the home facility and receive a baseball scholarship. You will have four seasons left of eligibility.

Non-Qualifier Requirements
You will be classified as a Non Qualifier if you fail to graduate from high school or do not meet the core-curriculum GPA and SAT/ACT scores required for a qualifier. If you are a Non-Qualifier, you cannot practice with the team, play games, or receive a baseball scholarship during your first year. You will have four seasons left of eligibility.

Division II
2005 and Later

If you enroll in a Division II college in 2005 or later and want to play baseball or receive an athletics scholarship during your first year, you must:

- Graduate from high school,
- Complete these 14 core courses:
    - 3 years of English
    - 2 years of math (algebra 1 or higher)
    - 2 years of natural or physical science (including one year of lab science if offered by your high school)
    - 2 extra years of English, math or natural or physical science
    - 2 years of social science
    - 3 years of extra core courses (from any category above, or foreign language, non-doctrinal religion or philosophy);
- Earn a 2.000 grade-point average or better in your core courses; and
- Earn a combined SAT score of 820 or an ACT sum score of 68.

There is no sliding scale in Division II.

NCAA DIVISION III

D-III schools tend to recruit regionally, do not offer scholarships, but comprise some of the most prestigious academic schools in the country. There are 301 D-III schools and none offer baseball scholarships, though many offer generous academic scholarships.

Academic Eligibility Requirements - Division III
D-III schools do not have standard requirements. Check with the individual schools that interest you for details.

NATIONAL ASSOCIATION OF INTERCOLLEGIATE ATHLETICS (NAIA)

The NAIA represents 180 four-year schools. Each NAIA school is allowed to award 12 full baseball scholarships. The National Association of Intercollegiate Athletics, an athletic league completely separate from the NCAA, began in 1937. The organization is divided into thirty-two districts representing the fifty states.

Contact Info
NAIA
23500 W. 105th St. - P.O. Box 1325
Olathe, KS 66051
Web: www.naia.org/
Phone: 913-791-0044

Academic Eligibility Requirements
You must meet two of the following three eligibility requirements:
- Graduate in the upper half of your high school class
- Earn a combined score of at least 860 on the SAT or 68 on the ACT
- Earn a 2.0 cumulative GPA (based on a 4.0 scale)

For a complete list of eligibility requirements, procedures, guidelines, and association by-laws, call the NAIA and ask to receive a copy of their manual, *A Guide for the College-Bound Athlete*.

NATIONAL JUNIOR COLLEGE ATHLETIC ASSOCIATION (NJCAA)

The NJCAA consists of 377 two-year programs representing three separate divisions (I, II, and III). D-I and D-II schools offer up to 24 scholarships. D-III schools do not offer scholarships.

If you yearn for the experience of living in a dorm, spending Saturday afternoons cheering for the home football team, and enjoying an active social life, you should choose a four-year school. If not, a junior college may be a perfect option for you. While most JCs offer a wide array of extracurricular activities, the students commute and many of them work full-time, so they have less time for social activities.

You have two options if you attend a JC. The first is called a Transfer Program, which enables you to leave school after one or two years and transfer your credits earned to a four-year school. The second option is called a Terminal Program, which earns you an associate's degree after attending school for two years.

Contact Info
NJCAA
1755 Telstar Dr.
Colorado Springs, CO 809920
Phone: 719-590-9788
Web: www.njcaa.org

Academic Requirements
JCs generally offer an open-door admission policy so you don't have to worry about getting in. However, you must meet one of the following requirements:
- Graduate from high school
- Receive a high school equivalency diploma
- Pass a national test such as the General Education Development Test (GED)

For a complete list of eligibility requirements, procedures, guidelines, and association by-laws, call the NJCAA and ask to receive a copy of their manual, *NJCAA Handbook & Casebook*.

Letter Of Intent
The NJCAA Letter of Intent is used to commit an individual to a specific institution for a period of one year and is only valid for NJCAA colleges. You may sign a Letter of Intent with both a NJCAA college and a NCAA college, but may not sign a Letter of Intent with two NJCAA colleges. If you sign a Letter of Intent with two NJCAA colleges, you will be ineligible for one year.

Benefits of Attending a Junior College

Attending a two-year junior or community college is a great option for many athletes. Here are some reasons why you may want to consider the JC route:

Your GPA, SAT/ACT, or Core Courses Did Not Meet the Four-Year Schools' Requirements

If you did not apply yourself academically in high school and your marks are not indicative of your full potential, you might be better off starting college with a year or two of JC and then transferring to a four-year school.

You Need another Year At Home before Going Away To School

If you feel that another year living at home would help ease the transition to a four-year college, then a local JC is a good option.

You Don't Want To Compete At Any Of The Four-Year Schools To Which You've been Accepted

If you got a late start preparing for college and are not happy with the schools you've been admitted to, a year of JC exposure may give you a better opportunity to fully explore all your four-year options.

Your Family Cannot Afford To Send You to a Four-Year School at This Time

Tuition at JCs is very inexpensive and athletic scholarships are more plentiful. Even if you don't receive a scholarship, you can attend most for only a couple of thousand dollars a year.

You Also Want To Work Full-Time

A JC is also a practical choice for students who need class schedules flexible enough to accommodate full-time jobs. The schools typically offer classes from 8 a.m. to 10 p.m. weekdays and on Saturday mornings to accommodate students with jobs.

8
FORMS YOU'LL NEED AND REFERENCES YOU'LL USE

In This Chapter

- Checklists to guide you through each year of high school in both baseball and academics
- Sample correspondence and profile
- Useful web sites
- Form to help you identify your top school
- Charts for figuring costs and your family contribution

This chapter serves as a catch-all for the topics that were covered earlier in the book. Here you'll find useful tools to help you through the recruiting process.

CHECKLIST

Freshman School Year & Summer

Academic
- ☐ Take the most challenging courses you can handle.
- ☐ Meet your guidance counselor and let him know of your desire to compete in college. Make sure he knows that you must meet the core course requirement.
- ☐ Work hard at school and strive for a 4.0 GPA.
- ☐ Learn to manage your time and develop good study habits.
- ☐ Visit any college campuses you can. The best choices are your parents' alma maters and the schools of relatives, siblings, and friends currently attending college.

Baseball
- ☐ Attend at least two local college games.
- ☐ Purchase instructional tapes to help you improve your skills.
- ☐ Play on a fall baseball team, if available.
- ☐ Stay in shape year round by running and lifting weights (ask your school's trainer for one).
- ☐ Follow an offseason throwing and hitting schedule (ask your high school coach for one).
- ☐ Attend a Christmas break camp if it does not conflict with your winter sports season.
- ☐ Play on your school's freshman, JV, or varsity baseball team.
- ☐ Attend showcase camps and play for competitive summer teams.

Sophomore School Year & Summer

Academic
- ☐ Make a commitment to improve your grades and take challenging courses.
- ☐ Meet with your guidance counselor to make sure you are taking classes to satisfy your core course requirement and staying on track.
- ☐ Hire a tutor, form a study group with your friends, and seek extra help from your teachers in order to improve your GPA.
- ☐ Start researching various careers in which you might have interest to give you an idea of potential college majors.
- ☐ Make a preliminary Target List. Include as many schools as possible.
- ☐ Take the PSAT in October so you know where you need to improve.
- ☐ Visit more college campuses.

Baseball
- ☐ Attend at least two college games from different divisions.
- ☐ Make unofficial visits to as many schools on your Target List as possible
- ☐ Play on a fall baseball team, if available.
- ☐ Stay in shape year round by running and lifting weights (ask your school's trainer for one).
- ☐ Follow an offseason throwing and hitting schedule (ask your high school coach for one).
- ☐ Attend a Christmas break camp if it does not conflict with your winter sports season.
- ☐ Play on your school's JV, or varsity baseball team.
- ☐ Attend showcase camps and play for competitive summer teams.

Junior School Year & Summer

Academic

- ☐ Make a commitment to improve your grades and take challenging courses.
- ☐ Start compiling a Target List of schools that interest you both academically and athletically. Consider the schools you have visited and draw on the experiences of your parents, siblings, and family friends.
- ☐ Meet with your guidance counselor to make sure you are taking classes to satisfy your core course requirements and to get advice on your Target List.
- ☐ Enroll in a prep course like Kaplan or Princeton Review to help you achieve the highest possible SAT/ACT score.
- ☐ Take the *USNews* web page survey to help identify schools that meet your needs.
- ☐ Speak with your parents and family friends about their college experiences.
- ☐ Review your Target List of schools monthly to remove or add schools.
- ☐ Read college catalogs and Web pages of schools you are considering.
- ☐ Take the PSAT again in October.
- ☐ Take the SAT/ACT in the spring.
- ☐ Consider enrolling in AP classes

Baseball

- ☐ Register with the NCAA Clearinghouse.
- ☐ Call each college division to request a copy of their student/athlete guide so you are familiar with all rules and regulations.
- ☐ Attend as many games of schools on your Target List as you can.
- ☐ Send letters of interest and your player profile to coaches on your Target List, preferably before your high school season starts.
- ☐ Ask your high school coach, summer league coach, and any other coaches or scouts who have seen you compete to send letters of recommendation to schools on your Target List.
- ☐ Complete and return college questionnaires promptly.
- ☐ Seek opinions from high school coaches and other qualified persons concerning your ability to play college baseball.
- ☐ Make unofficial visits to as many schools on your Target List as possible.
- ☐ Meet with the head coach of any school you visit.
- ☐ Publish your personal web site and promote it to college coaches.
- ☐ Produce a highlight video when you are playing at your peak - if possible, in June. Send the tape to schools interested in recruiting you, if they request it.
- ☐ Seek national exposure by attending showcase camps, playing in high-profile summer leagues and tournaments, and attending summer camps at your top-choice schools
- ☐ Play on a fall baseball team, if available, that travels to the country's top showcases.
- ☐ Attend a Christmas break camp if it does not conflict with your winter sport season.
- ☐ Stay in shape year round by running and lifting weights (ask your school's trainer to design a program for you).
- ☐ Follow an offseason throwing and hitting schedule (ask your high school coach for one).
- ☐ Play on your school's varsity baseball team.
- ☐ Play for the most competitive summer team you can find. Make sure it travels to tournaments that attract attention from college coaches.
- ☐ Seek invitations to the country's top summer showcases.
- ☐ Send coaches on your Target List your summer league, showcase, and tournament schedule.
- ☐ Attend a pro tryout camp (a recommendation from a pro scout carries a lot of weight).

Senior School Year & Summer

Academic

- ☐ Retake the SAT/ACT.
- ☐ Compare your GPA with your SAT/ACT score and the qualifier index.
- ☐ Retake the SAT/ACT if your scores need improvement.
- ☐ In September, request a copy of "Meeting College Costs" from your guidance office to determine how much money you need for college.
- ☐ Ask for teacher recommendations.
- ☐ Finalize your Target List and apply to these schools.
- ☐ Meet all application and financial aid deadlines.
- ☐ Evaluate your college options and consider scholarship and financial offers.
- ☐ Inform each college to which you've been accepted of your final decision.
- ☐ Fill out your FAFSA form as soon as you make your final decision

Baseball

- ☐ Call each college division to request a copy of their student/athlete guide so you are familiar with all rules and regulations (the guides are updated yearly so you want to stay abreast of any changes).
- ☐ Make unofficial and official visits to schools on your Target List.
- ☐ Play on a fall baseball team, if available, that travels to the country's top showcases.
- ☐ Attend a Christmas break camp if it does not conflict with your winter sport season.
- ☐ Stay in shape year round by running and lifting weights (ask your school's trainer to design a program for you).
- ☐ Follow an offseason throwing and hitting schedule (ask your high school coach for one).
- ☐ Play on your school's varsity baseball team.
- ☐ Play for a competitive summer team so you are ready for your college fall tryout.

CORRESPONDENCE

The purpose of this section is to help you think of ideas for your correspondence with college coaches. Do not copy any of these letters word-for-word. Make sure you write your own versions so you stand out from the crowd. Also, many coaches are familiar with this guide and it will look bad for you if they notice you plagiarized it.

Tips

- Type long letters but handwrite shorter ones if your writing is neat and legible. It will be more personal than if you type them (you can type your Player Profile).
- Individualize your letters - do not send the same version to multiple schools. If a coach feels like you sent a bulk mailing, he will not give your letter as much attention.
- Use stationery to give your correspondence a professional appearance. You can design your own version on a computer using a nice font. Include your name, address, phone, and e-mail.
- Do not call or mail letters to a college coach at his house unless he gives you permission. It's rude and you may annoy him. Always use the coach's office as your contact point.
- Send letters promptly. A thank-you note received the day after a meeting makes a much better impression than one received two weeks later.

Coaches evaluate the "little things" too!
Bob Temple, VarisityPages.com

Everything you do, and everything you send to a college coach, reflects on you. This includes some of the "little things" that many people may not think about.

My company recently needed to hire a large number of writers to help out with a specific project. To do this, I placed an advertisement for "freelance writers" on a popular job-search site. The response to the ad was tremendous. There were hundreds of writers who sent in their resumes (just like there might be hundreds of athletes interested in being recruited by a college coach). In going through those communications, I weeded out candidates based primarily on their qualifications, of course. But "little things" also played a role.

One such little thing was a particular writer's email address. Before I even got a chance to look at his cover letter or resume, I noticed that his email address was a reference to his favorite alcoholic beverage. When he created this email address, he probably thought it was funny. But using it in a business context was inappropriate. So, if your primary email address might give a negative impression (surferdude@xyz.com or bigmanoncampus@xyz.com, for example), you might want to consider changing it, or using a different one to communicate with coaches.

Bob Temple is a sports writer who has covered all the major professional sports leagues, major college sports, and high school sports throughout a 19-year writing career. He's also authored seven Internet-related books (two on sports topics) and more than 20 children's non-fiction books (eight on sports topics).

Letter of Interest
Purpose: To let a college coach know you are interested in playing for his baseball team. Discuss your academic interests and request literature on the school and team.

Athlete Profile
Purpose: To highlight your academic and athletic accomplishments in an easy-to-read format. Include personal, athletic and academic information, references, and photo of you in your baseball uniform. This should accompany the Letter of Interest.

Letter Accompanying a Highlight Video
Purpose: To introduce your highlight video and encourage the coach to watch it. Mention that you are sending the video because the coach asked for one. Do not send a video unless a coach requests it.

Thank You Note after a Campus Visit
Purpose: To thank a coach for taking the time to meet with you, discuss the possibility of playing for his team, and to let him know you are still interested in being recruited. Include specific examples of something pertaining to your meeting so the coach remembers you.

Letter Providing New Information
Purpose: To inform a coach of new developments and reinforce your desire to be recruited. You can send a copy of your game schedule, let the coach know that you will be competing in a national event, or that you just made the Dean's List.

JASON KLINE

10324 Town Walk Dr.
Yorktown Heights, NY 10598
Phone: 914-555-1000   E-Mail: shortstop7@aol.com

August 28, 2006

Mr. Keith Kessinger
Head Baseball Coach
Carson-Newman College
2130 Branner Avenue
Jefferson City, TN 37760

Dear Coach Kessinger:

    After I graduate from Yorktown H.S. this June, I am interested in attending Carson-Newman College. My goal is to graduate with a Pre-Med degree from your prestigious McCarthur School. I am writing to express interest in attending your school and more specifically, playing middle infield for your baseball team next year.

    As a three-year captain of my high school team, I have developed the skills and leadership ability to contribute to your nationally ranked squad. This past season I was the team captain and was voted All-Section MVP for hitting .325 with a .977 fielding percentage.

    My interest in Carson-Newman College has always been strong - I have had the opportunity to attend seven of your games (including last year's amazing 7-6 come-from-behind win against Lincoln Memorial). In fact, two alumni from my high school, Jim Nicholson and Spencer Davis, played for your team in the mid-1990s.

    Attached is a Player Profile that details my academic and athletic accomplishments. You'll notice that I take my studies just as seriously as I do baseball, and I'm confident that I will represent your program with distinction. I even produced a four-minute highlight tape. Please call or e-mail if you want me to send a copy.

    Please add my name to your prospect list and send me information about Carson-Newman's baseball program. I would especially like to see a copy of your media guide.

    Good luck this spring in my improving last season's tremendous 34-14 record. I know this is your year to upset top-seeded Tennessee Tech for the South Atlantic Conference title.

    Good luck this season.

    Go Eagles!

Sincerely yours,

Jason

Jason Kline

JASON KLINE   SS/2B   CLASS '07

Address: 10324 Town Walk Dr.
Phone: 914-555-1000
E-mail: shortstop7@aol.com
DOB: June 24, 1988
Height: 6'4"
Weight: 165 lbs.
SS#   102-24-2422

ACADEMIC
High School: Yorktown High School
                17 Green Road
                Yorktown Heights, NY 10598
                914-232-9444
Graduation: Class of 2007
GPA: 3.8 GPA (on a 4.0 scale)
Class Rank: Top 10%
SAT: 1900 Total (600 math, 640 verbal, 660 writing)
Honors: National Merit Scholar
                2nd place County Science Fair Competition
                Student Volunteer of the Month - Mothers Against Drunk Driving
Counselor: Jim Ryan (ext. 343)

HIGH SCHOOL BASEBALL
Coach   Jim Dobbs (ext. 432)
Awards: Varsity letterman - '04-'06
                First Team All-Section - '05
                Team Captain & All-Section MVP - '06
2006 Stats: .325 BA, .584 on-base-percentage, .977 fielding percentage
Other Sports: 3 year football (All-League), 2 years wrestling (All-Conference)

SUMMER BASEBALL
Coach: Jim Zollo - Phone: 914-232-9848
                American Legion - Post 187, 12 River Run, Rochester, NY 10222
Awards: All-Tournament Selection - Fourth of July Summer Bash
                Tournament MVP - Atlanta Memorial Classic
2006 Stats: .404 BA, .590 on-base percentage, .968 fielding percentage
Camps: Baseball Factory - Los Angeles, CA (Aug., '05 & '06)
                Powerhouse Academy - Jupiter, FL (Dec., '05)
                Frozen Ropes - White Plains, NY (Feb., '06)

REFERENCES
Pro Scout   Jim Haas - Texas Rangers (718-232-9453)
Former Pro   Lenny Coleman - New York Mets AAA (212-454-2234
Teacher   Deborah Klein - (ext. 232) - English AP
Employer   Calvin Hobbs - McDonalds (718-343-3453)
Volunteer Mgr. Stacey Jackson - Mothers Against Drunk Driving (718-343-9343)

SAMPLE LETTERS

Handwrite these letters on your stationery and use the same layout as in the Letter of Interest:

Letter Accompanying Highlight Video

Dear Coach Kessinger:

Here is a copy of my highlight video, which you requested. It lasts four minutes so it will not take you a long time to evaluate my skills. I'm confident you'll see for yourself that I can be a valuable contributor to your Eagles Baseball team.

If you would like to see me play in person, I have just been selected to participate at the Baseball Factory USA Junior Olympic Tournament College, June 20-30, in Jupiter, Florida. In addition, I have recently been taking lessons with Steve Bonner, a former college player at U. of Louisville and now a pro scout with the Baltimore Orioles. Coach Bonner (718-232-9834) can answer questions about my ability.

Thanks for taking the time to watch my tape.

Thank You Note after a Campus Visit

Dear Coach Kessinger:

Thank you for taking time to meet with me during my visit to Carson-Newman College last Saturday. I really enjoyed touring the campus, attending a science class, and speaking with you about your baseball team. It gave me a great glimpse of what I can expect at college next fall. I cannot wait!

I am glad I got a chance to see your team play against Middle Georgia. You're right...your team sure can hit! I was impressed with the talent of your squad, the team unity, and competitive spirit of your players. I can definitely see myself wearing the Blue & Gold!

Thanks again for your hospitality and for your interest in recruiting me.

Letter Providing New Information

Dear Coach Kessinger:

I want to let you know that my high school baseball team will be competing at the Pinstripe Classic in Homestead, Florida, April 7-10. If any of your assistant coaches are covering the event, I'd really appreciate it if they could watch some of our games. I wear No. 7, play second base, and bat leadoff. Enclosed is the schedule.

By the way, I just found out that I made the Dean's List for the third semester in a row, and my research project on solar energy won third prize in our county science fair. My hard work is paying off!

Thanks again for considering me for your 2006 recruiting class.

INTERNET SITES

The Web offers a wealth of college-related resources, from free test-prep courses to loan calculators to statistics on campus crime. Nevertheless, you should surf carefully. Some sites accept fees from colleges to list their schools prominently. Others require you to register and will sell your personal information to marketers if you neglect to sign complicated privacy agreements.

Moreover, when researching colleges online it's important to dig deep and think critically. Many colleges have spent thousands of dollars on fancy web sites that are little more than glitzy ads.

College Board (www.Collegeboard.com)
Collegeboard.com is one of the most comprehensive sites. It produces a customized roster of schools for students who answer questions on everything from dorms to school size. The site also contains other important information relating to the SATs and AP tests. For instance, the site lists schools that allow students with one year's worth of AP or International Baccalaureate credits to skip a year of college. In addition, it includes a free, searchable scholarship database called "LikeFinder."

US News & World Report (www.Usnews.com)
Their search creates a list of potential schools based on your answers to questions about cost, geographic location, major, and several other preferences. The site features college rankings so you can identify schools according to the criteria that matter most to you, such as student-to-faculty ratio or acceptance rate. Another tool is the personality quiz. Rate the validity of 80 statements, including "I want to be able to contribute to society someday" and "friends and I enjoy discussing intellectual ideas," to find out the kinds of colleges where you'll feel at home. Need help whittling down your list? Chat with counselors and other experts on the Forum or compare the stats of up to four schools.

Once a search engine has spit out a list of possible schools, you typically can click straight to each college's home page. In the past couple of years, these pages have become a popular source of information about colleges, offering course catalogs, sample financial aid packages, and virtual campus tours.

But students should bear in mind that much of the material on these sites is promotional. The Internet Guide for college-Bound Students, encourages students to browse not only the "official" pages, like the virtual tour, but to ferret out "unofficial" information as well.

Princeton Review (www.Review.com)
More hip, but more commercial, is Princeton Review's site. Its Counselor-O-Matic poses glib questions about your academic performance and interests. Then the site produces a list of colleges divided into "safety," "good match," and "reach" schools. It also has college admissions discussion boards, but you have to register to participate.

Apply On-Line
Once you have your final Target List, the Internet can make the process of applying a little easier. Many college sites have applications that either can be printed and filled out by hand or completed electronically. In addition, you can log on to one of several sites devoted to E-applications. In most cases, the services are free, although students still have to pay an application fee to the schools.

Some of them, like www.collegelink.com (a Web partner of US News Online), www.xap.com, and www.collegenet.com, host hundreds of colleges' applications, which can be filled out and submitted electronically.

Students also can turn to www.commonapp.org for a generic form, called the Common Application, which is accepted by 209 colleges.

But don't let the relative ease of applying electronically be your downfall. Too often, students who would take care with a paper form hurry through online applications. If you decide to apply online, be sure to have a parent or teacher read over your essays before you hit the submit button.

Financial Aid (www.ed.gov/studentaid)
One of the first sites you will want to visit in your search for college funds is the Department of Education's federal student financial aid home page. The government gives grants, loans, and work-study assistance to more than 10 million students each year, and if you want to be among their ranks, you'll need to fill out their Federal Student Aid, or FAFSA. The site provides so much detailed information, however, that it can put you to sleep.

For a jazzier discussion of federal programs, check out http://www.finaid.org/. This site also offers calculators to help you figure out how much you will get from the government and how long it will take to pay the loans back. While numerous sites provide searchable scholarship databases, stay clear of those that charge you money or "guarantee" that you'll win a scholarship; scholarship scams are prevalent.

Loans (www.wiredscholar.com)
Sallie Mae, the largest private education loan company, runs one of the best funding information sites. Easy to navigate and without registration requirements, the site has a database of hundreds of thousands of scholarships worth over a billion dollars. Why does the firm offer the site? To acquire new loan customers. In other words, if you don't find a scholarship, a private loan is just a click away.

Scholarship Database (www.fastweb.com)
With over 600,000 awards, Fastweb is one of the most aggressive in updating its scholarship database. To use the search, however, you must submit to a lengthy registration process that includes solicitations that pop up between questions. Fastweb sells registered users' names to banks and universities, and those who don't want their names released must indicate this at the beginning of the registration process.

Athletic Scholarships (www.athleticscholarships.net)
Their athletic scholarship recruiting service can help you apply for college athletic scholarships. Our service covers all NCAA and NAIA sports.

Social Life (www.collegenews.com)
To get the skinny on the social life at a particular college, check out this site. It also has a complete listing of college newspapers.

Proofreading Application essays (www.essayedge.com)
Also worth a click is EssayEdge, a site that offers a wealth of free material on writing college essays. For a fee, their experts also will read and edit your essay.

Test Prep (www.testu.com)
TestU charges $50 for an online program based of your strengths and weaknesses. www.Number2.com takes the democratization of test prep further by offering a free interactive course.

Not to be outdone, last year both Kaplan and Princeton Review introduced online courses, as well as free mini-courses. And even the College Board-which sponsors the SAT-has gotten in on the act with free and low-cost test prep.

Crime Reports (www.ope.ed.gov/security)
This is a good source to find out about a school's safety record. Think critically about what you read. When institutions report crime data they use different definitions of offenses so some direct comparisons among campuses may not be valid.

College Net (www.collegenet.com)
A matching service that helps you find your ideal school and on-line applications from over 1,500 colleges.

Preparing Your Child for College (www.ed.gov/studentaid)
Helps your parents with general college concerns.

Peterson's Education Center (www.petersons.com)
A leading provider of college entrance exam preparation.

College Bound Magazine (www.collegebound.net)
Informative magazine articles to help with issues facing incoming freshmen. Subscriptions available.

College Apps (www.collegeapps.com)
Collegeapps.com shows college-bound students how to personalize that very sterile college application form and market themselves to gain admission.

Collegenet (www.collegenet.com)
Provides here for your convenience over 1500 customized Internet admissions applications built for college and university programs. When applying to more than one program you save redundant typing since common data automatically travels from form to form.

Get Recruited (www.get-recruited.com)
Helps make the college recruiting process work for both students and institutions of higher education. Brings students together with colleges, universities, graduate schools, and professional schools and helps them identify the scholarships and financial aid for which they may qualify.

A-Game (www.a-game.com)
This site is here to help you play your A-Game- not just in your sport, but also in the classroom. We want to help you take advantage of the opportunities- and avoid the dangers- in sports, school, and life.

College Link (www.collegelink.com)
Assists you with your college search, applying, and making your final college decision.

Financial Aid Information Page (www.finaid.org)
Answers all questions about financial aid, loans, scholarships, and military aid.

Scholarships (www.scholarships.com)
Scholarship finder and general information about financial aid.

Financial Aid (www.fafsa.ed.gov)
An on-line version of the Free Application for Federal Student Aid

Mapping Your Future (www.mapping-your-future.org)
Helps you plan a career after college.

Career Resource Center (www.careers.org)
Assists with career advice and planning.

National Student Loan Data System (www.nslds.ed.gov)
The U.S. Department of Education's central database for student aid that receives data from schools, agencies that guarantee loans, the Direct Loan program, the Pell Grant program, and others.

American Baseball Coaches Association (www.abca.org)
Even though this site is geared to college coaches, it features instructional articles, national poll results, and interesting feature stories.

High School Baseball Web (www.hsbaseballweb.com)
Comprehensive information geared to high school players featuring recruiting articles, how to information, interviews with college coaches, message boards, and listing of over 1,000 high school baseball team websites.

National High School Baseball Coaches Association (www.baseballcoaches.org)
Provides services and recognition for high school coaches and helps promote and represent high school baseball.

National Collegiate Athletic Association (www.ncaa.org)
Represents 777 four-year schools in three separate divisions (I, II, and III).

National Athletic of Intercollegiate Athletics (www.naia.org)
Represents 180 four-year schools.

National Junior College Athletic Association (www.njcaa.org)
Represents 377 two-year programs representing three separate divisions (I, II, and III).

ONLINE COLLEGE QUESTIONNAIRES

Filling out an online college questionnaire is a quick and effective way for you to show your interest in a particular school. Online questionnaires allow potential student athletes to give coaches a brief overview of who they are and what they want to accomplish.

Although questionnaires can be filled out quickly online, it is important that you not take it for granted. These forms are seen as a reflection of who you are, so answer each question with well-thought-out answers.

Guidelines to Keep In Mind When Filling Out Online College Questionnaires

- **Proofread at least twice.** By putting extra effort into assuring the copy you send a perspective coach is well written and error-free, you are sending a message that you are detail-oriented, responsible and motivated.

- **It is never too early.** Fill in questionnaires as soon as you place a school on your Target List. The earlier you complete a questionnaire, the sooner you get your name around at your top choice schools.

- **Do your homework.** Where possible on the questionnaire, demonstrate your strong interest in the school. Include specific classes, professors or other attributes of the college or university that interest you.

COLLEGE INFORMATION SHEET

The best way to keep your college materials organized is to print this sheet for each school on your Target List. Place each sheet - along with any school catalogs or other information you receive - inside a file folder. Write the school's name on the outside of the folder.

General

School_____ Division:_____

Address_____City_____State_____Zip_____

Admissions Dept Phone_____Web Page_____

Academics

Academic Rating: ❑ Most Competitive ❑ Average ❑ Less Competitive ❑ Not Competitive

Potential Major/Departments of interest_____

Prestige of degree: ❑ Very Prestigious ❑ Average ❑ Not Prestigious

Undergraduate Enrollment_____Faculty:Student Ratio_____

Average GPA of accepted applicants_____Average SAT/ACT scores_____

Likelihood of being accepted: ❑ Safety School ❑ Likely ❑ Reach

Conversation notes with admission department (include date & what you discussed)
_____
_____
_____

Baseball

Head Coach_____Recruiting Coordinator_____

Assistant Coach(es)_____

Athletic Office Phone_____E-mail addresses_____

Coach's interest: ❑ Recruiting me heavily ❑ Slight interest ❑ No discussions yet ❑ None

Roster players at my position_____How many recruited at my position_____

Likelihood of making the team: ❑ Definitely ❑ Maybe ❑ Slim Chance

Copyright 2008 Mazz Marketing   203--260-4932   Wayne@WayneMazzoni.com

Been to a game?_____ Compete on TV? _____

Does coach want me to red-shirt?   ❏ Yes   ❏ No   Graduation rate of athletes:_____

Scholarship offered?   ❏ No   ❏ Yes - Amount_____

Competitive schedule?   ❏ Yes   ❏ No   Overnight trips: ❏ Yes ❏ No

Offered an Official Visit: ❏ No   ❏ Yes - When_____

Unofficial Visit planned?   ❏ No   ❏ Yes - When_____

Baseball Facilities (fields, practice facility, weight room) ❏ Excellent   ❏ Average   ❏ Poor

Strength of team/schedule: ❏ Excellent   ❏ Average   ❏ Weak

Conversation notes with coaches (include date & what you discussed)
_____
_____

Finances

Tuition_____ Room & Board_____ Transportation To/From Home _____

How much of a financial aid/ scholarship package do I need to afford this school?_____

Conversation notes with financial aid department (include date & what you discussed):
_____
_____

Other Considerations

Housing: ❏ On-campus dorm ❏ Off-campus apartment

Campus Life: ❏ Lots of activities ❏ Average ❏ Little to do

Greek Life: ❏ Big ❏ Average ❏ Small ❏ None

Transportation home: ❏ Fly - Duration of trip_____   ❏ Drive - Duration of trip_____

Friends, relatives, or high school alumni who have gone to this school:_____

Would I be happy at this school if I didn't play baseball? ❏ Yes ❏ No

IDENTIFY YOUR #1 SCHOOL

If you have trouble selecting a school that you want to attend, complete this exercise after you receive your acceptance letters.

1. Specify how important each of the following criteria is to you by checking in one of the three boxes labeled "Very," "Somewhat" or "Not." This will help focus your decision.
2. Rank what you feel is "Very Important" to you on a scale of 1-5 (5 being best).
3. Add up all the rankings. If this doesn't clearly identify your #1 choice, then you can rank all the criteria that you feel are "Somewhat Important."

IMPORTANCE TO ME?			CRITERIA	SCHOOL #1 (_____)	SCHOOL #2 (_____)	SCHOOL #3 (_____)
Very	Somewhat	Not				
			Academics			
☐	☐	☐	School's reputation	_____	_____	_____
☐	☐	☐	Fields of study	_____	_____	_____
☐	☐	☐	Prestige of degree	_____	_____	_____
☐	☐	☐	Professors	_____	_____	_____
☐	☐	☐	Class size	_____	_____	_____
☐	☐	☐	Alumni network	_____	_____	_____
☐	☐	☐	Small enrollment	_____	_____	_____
☐	☐	☐	In-State	_____	_____	_____
☐	☐	☐	Out-of-State	_____	_____	_____
☐	☐	☐	Athletic Tutoring	_____	_____	_____
			Baseball			
☐	☐	☐	Baseball Scholarship	_____	_____	_____
☐	☐	☐	Chance to Start	_____	_____	_____
☐	☐	☐	High-profile team/conf	_____	_____	_____
☐	☐	☐	Transfer opportunities	_____	_____	_____
☐	☐	☐	Caliber of team	_____	_____	_____
☐	☐	☐	Competitive schedule	_____	_____	_____
☐	☐	☐	Coaching staff	_____	_____	_____
☐	☐	☐	Baseball facilities	_____	_____	_____
☐	☐	☐	Pro Scout Exposure	_____	_____	_____
☐	☐	☐	Grad rates of players	_____	_____	_____
			Other			
☐	☐	☐	My parents approve	_____	_____	_____
☐	☐	☐	Location	_____	_____	_____
☐	☐	☐	Climate	_____	_____	_____
☐	☐	☐	Greek life	_____	_____	_____
☐	☐	☐	Distance from home	_____	_____	_____
☐	☐	☐	Campus events	_____	_____	_____
☐	☐	☐	Social life	_____	_____	_____
☐	☐	☐	Meet new people	_____	_____	_____
☐	☐	☐	Out-of-pocket cost	_____	_____	_____
			Grand Total	_____	_____	_____

COST OF COLLEGE COMPARISON

EXPENSES	SCHOOL #1	SCHOOL #2	SCHOOL #3
	(_____)	(_____)	(_____)
Tuition & Fees	_____	_____	_____
Room & Board	_____	_____	_____
Books & Supplies	_____	_____	_____
Personal Expenses	_____	_____	_____
Transportation	_____	_____	_____
Other	_____	_____	_____
TOTAL EXPENSES	_____	_____	_____
TOTAL FINANCIAL AID	_____	_____	_____
YOUR ANNUAL COST	_____	_____	_____

(Total Expenses minus Total Financial Aid)

ESTIMATED FAMILY CONTRIBUTION

This chart provides an approximation of how much financial aid departments will expect your family to contribute toward your college expenses each year. The figures are based on only one parent working, no other siblings in college, and no unusual financial circumstances. You should also add a $700-$1,000 student contribution to the final amount. These figures are only estimates. Your actual contribution may vary.

2005-2006 Estimated Parent Contribution

Net Assets of $25,000

Family Size	3	4	5	6
Income Before Taxes				
$20,000	$0	$0	$0	$0
$30,000	$1,060	$230	$0	$0
$40,000	$2,690	$1,900	$1,160	$290
$50,000	$4,680	$3,600	$2,750	$1,910
$60,000	$7,550	$5,990	$4,780	$3,620
$70,000	$10,950	$9,260	$7,680	$6,020
$80,000	$14,210	$12,660	$11,080	$9,290

Net Assets of $50,000

Family Size	3	4	5	6
Income Before Taxes				
$20,000	$0	$0	$0	$0
$30,000	$1,380	$560	$0	$0
$40,000	$3,050	$2,220	$1,480	$610
$50,000	$5,180	$4,030	$3,120	$2,230
$60,000	$8,240	$6,580	$5,280	$4,050
$70,000	$11,640	$9,950	$8,370	$6,610
$80,000	$14,910	$13,350	$11,770	$9,990

Net Assets of $100,000

Family Size	3	4	5	6
Income Before Taxes				
$20,000	$1,000	$130	$0	$0
$30,000	$2,700	$1,880	$1,100	$230
$40,000	$4,760	$3,670	$2,810	$1,930
$50,000	$7,660	$6,090	$4,860	$3,690
$60,000	$11,060	$9,370	$7,790	$6,120
$70,000	$14,460	$12,770	$11,190	$9,400
$80,000	$16,560	$16,170	$14,590	$12,810

Please note that the charts assume the following:
- Two parents in the family, both employed and earning equal wages.
- Income only from employment.
- The family has no unusual financial circumstances, such as high medical expenses.
- The standard deduction is used when calculating taxes on the 1040 form.
- One child is enrolled in college when college expenses must be paid.
- Calculations are according to the "federal methodology," which is used to determine federal aid, and which some schools follow (VSAC uses a slightly different methodology for determining Vermont grants); the federal methodology excludes the value of a family's home or farm.
- Calculations are based on 2004 income and apply to the 2005-2006 academic year.

BOTTOM OF THE NINTH

Different people can use the forms and checklists in this section at different stages of the process. Begin with the checklists at the beginning of the chapter. Even if you're a junior already, go back through the freshman and sophomore checklists and determine if you completed all the items. Then bring yourself up to date to your current class.

Begin working on your correspondence. Check out some of the Web sites listed, and use the other forms as appropriate.

GLOSSARY OF TERMS

ACT A curriculum-based college admissions test. The multiple choice questions that test English, Mathematics, Reading, and Science Reasoning on the ACT are a measure of what you've learned in your high school classes rather than aptitude or IQ. Most U.S. colleges accept ACT results.

Advanced Placement Courses (AP) High school courses that can result in college credit, depending on your final exam score. College admissions officers generally look upon AP courses favorably as evidence of a challenging high school program.

Amateurism To be eligible to play college sports, students must maintain their amateur status.

Athletic Scholarship A form of financial aid that can be used to pay for tuition and fees, room and board, and books. It can be guaranteed for only one year at a time and must be renewed each year. Many coaches will verbally commit to and honor a four- or five-year scholarship even though they cannot put it in writing.

Award Letter A statement sent to you by colleges that have accepted you which recaps the amount and type of aid the college can offer.

Blue-Chip Recruit A highly sought-after high school athlete who attracts the attention of a wide variety of high-profile college coaches and pro scouts. This gifted player possesses outstanding athletic ability, a tremendous work ethic, and generally excellent academic marks.

Booster This person is usually a wealthy alumnus of the school with close ties to the athletic department. You will be ineligible for college athletics if you have any recruiting contact with boosters or alumni not employed by the college.

Bylaw 14.3 NCAA D-I and D-II legislation that requires you to meet a minimum GPA, SAT/ACT scores, take certain core courses, and graduate from high school before you can play college sports.

California Community Colleges Or CCC A small college division featuring 14 junior colleges in California. These schools do not offer scholarships.

Clearinghouse The organization responsible for certifying the academic eligibility for practice, competition and financial aid of all prospective student-athletes for Division I and Division II.

College Board A not-for-profit organization that administers many standardized tests including the PSAT, SAT, SAT II, and AP. Additionally, the College Board offers official test prep materials, a scholarship search, a personal inventory tool, and educational loans.

Commercial Loans or Private/Alternative Loans Commercial loans are available through several financial services providers. To qualify, you must pass a credit check, and the interest rate will be higher than that of a Direct or FFEL Stafford or Perkins Loan. For these reasons, it is wise to investigate low-interest, federally-sponsored options before applying for a commercial loan. In addition, beware of scholarship scams that are simply commercial loans in disguise.

Community College See Junior College

Contacts Any face-to-face meeting in excess of a greeting between you and a college coach or member of the athletic department. You may only be contacted off campus after July 1 before your senior year. Coaches may not contact you off campus more than three times.

Contact Period During this time, a college coach may have in-person contact with a student and/or the student's parents on or off the college's campus. The coach may also watch a student play or visit the student's high school. Students may visit the college campus and coaches may write or telephone students during this period.

Co-op An education that integrates classroom study with paid, supervised work experiences. These jobs are part or full-time and may lead to academic credit.

Core Courses Specified college preparatory courses that you need to take while in high school in order to be an eligible NCAA recruit.

Dead Period A period of time when a college coach may not have any in-person contact with a student or his or her family. The coach may write or call the student or the student's parents during this time.

Direct Expenses The total cost of tuition and fees, room and board, and books.

Early Signing Period One week in mid-November during which you can sign a National Letter of Intent.

Expected Family Contribution (EFC) The total you are expected to contribute toward the cost of college. The federal government determines the amount of your EFC based on the information you supply on the FAFSA and the total cost of attendance for the college of your choice. The total cost includes tuition, room and board, books, transportation, and other personal expenses. You will fill out the FAFSA each year, which may alter the EFC for each year of college.

Electronic Application An alternative to traditional paper applications, electronic applications can take several forms. Some schools allow you to print application forms from their Web site or a CD-ROM, which you can fill in by hand and mail to the admissions office. Other schools support online applications that you can fill out and submit over the web. If you decide to apply electronically, you will not have to wait to receive materials in the mail. Best of all, applying electronically will get your application in the hands of admissions officers sooner.

Evaluations Any off-campus activity used to assess your athletic ability. A coach may evaluate you at your high school or any other venue. NCAA D-III schools are not permitted to arrange an evaluation of you.

Financial Aid Package Each college has its own custom package, which may include federal and state grants, independent sources, school scholarships, student loans, and on-campus jobs. This provides you with a comparison guide among schools on your Target List.

Free Application For Federal Student Aid (FAFSA) The FAFSA is used to apply for federal student financial aid, including grants, loans, and work-study. In addition, it is used by most schools to award non-federal student financial aid. The form is a summary of your family's financial situation including income, debt, and assets for both you and your parents. You will have to fill out the FAFSA every year that you are in college.

Family Contribution The amount of money your family is expected to pay toward the Student Expense Budget. This amount is a fixed sum determined by the Federal Methodology and it will be the same regardless of what school you apply to.

Fellowships Available to students in most disciplines and sponsored by colleges and a broad range of organizations and institutions. Fellowships offered by organizations are often allocated in monthly stipends and can usually be used at any university. Fellowships are more common at the graduate level, but some undergraduate scholarships do exist. Additionally, there may be grant and fellowship money available for specific research projects or study abroad. Contact your major department, financial aid office, or career center for more information.

Federal Family Education Loan Program (FFEL) Low-interest education loans made by private lenders to students and parents. These loans may be either subsidized or unsubsidized, and there are several repayment plans available.

Financial Aid Any type of assistance used to help you meet college costs. It is divided into two categories: Gift Aid (athletic and academic scholarships and grants), and Self-Help Aid (loans and work study).

Federal Supplemental Educational Opportunity Grants (FSEOG) Government-sponsored, college-administered loans awarded to exceptionally needy students. Eligibility is determined by the federal government and the program gives priority to students receiving federal support.

Full Athletic Scholarship Or Full Ride Terms used when the college pays 100% of the expenses. These are rare and are usually given only to "blue-chip" athletes.

General Educational Development Test (GED) The GED may take the place of high-school graduation under certain conditions. If a student has the GED, he or she must still have the required number of core courses, the required grade-point average and the required ACT or SAT score.

Grant Aid This is the most sought-after type of financial aid because it does not have to be paid back. You may receive grant aid on the basis of either need or merit, and it may come from your school or the federal government. Federal grants include the need-based Pell and Federal Supplemental Educational Opportunity (FSEOG) grants.

Grayshirt A student who is recruited out of high school, but who delays full-time enrollment in college for a term or terms

Good Academic Standing Maintaining at least a C average while in college.

Home School A student who does not attend a traditional high school. A student who has been educated at home must register with the clearing-house like any other student.

Hook When you write your admissions essays, you'll want to engage your readers quickly. Using your "hook," a unique personal trait or experience, is one way to achieve this goal. If you are a dedicated and accomplished cellist or have trekked through the Himalayas, these might make good starting points for college essays. Your hook will be something about you that is unique and interesting.

Hope Credit A nonrefundable federal income tax credit equal to all of the first $1,000 out-of-pocket payments for qualified tuition and related expenses and 50% of the second $1,000, for a maximum $1,500 per student, per year. The Hope credit applies to the first two years of post-secondary education. You may not claim both the Hope Credit and the Lifetime Learning Credit (see below).

Indirect Expenses The total cost of transportation to and from school, incidental expenses, and supplies.

Ivy League The athletic conference that boasts academic powerhouses Brown, Columbia, Cornell, Dartmouth, Harvard, Penn, Princeton, and Yale. Acceptance to an Ivy League school is considered the brass ring of the application process, although many argue that an equal, if not better, education can be achieved at many non-Ivy League schools.

Junior College Or JC Or Juco Represents all two-year schools including community colleges. These schools provide college courses for recent high school graduates and adults in their communities. JCs generally have fewer admissions requirements than four-year institutions and courses typically cost less than comparable courses at four-year schools. Many students use JC as a springboard to a four-year college or university.

Lab Sciences High school science courses which supplement textbook study with hands-on experimentation. Examples include biology, chemistry, and physics. Other courses, such as economics, may be considered scientific disciplines, but do not qualify as lab sciences. Consult your guidance counselor or your prospective college's admissions office for further details.

Late Signing Period One week in mid-April during which you can sign a National Letter of Intent.

Letter Of Intent Or LOI A four-page contract, administered by the Collegiate Commissioners Association, that commits you to attend a specific college. If you change your mind after signing the letter, you must be mutually released from your commitment by the old school and your new school. In addition, you cannot play for one year and you lose a year of eligibility. This is a serious contract that should not be taken lightly.

Lifetime Learning Credit The Lifetime Learning Credit may be claimed for your tuition and related expenses on your parents' tax returns. Through 2002, the amount that may be claimed as a credit is equal to 20% of the taxpayer's first $5,000 of out-of-pocket qualified tuition and related expenses for all the students in the family for a maximum of $1,000. Individuals with modified adjusted gross incomes of $50,000 or more and joint filers with modified adjusted gross incomes of $100,000 or more are not eligible for the Lifetime Learning Credit.

Likely Letter A letter sent to an athletic scholarship recipient in the fall or early winter that lets him know the likelihood of being accepted to the school and the probable size of the financial package he will receive.

Merit-Based Aid Or Merit Scholarships Any form of financial aid not based on demonstrated financial need. Each school and/or its alumni associations and wealthy benefactors generally grant merit-based aid, which can take the form of grants, athletic or academic scholarships, or loans on favorable terms. You may qualify for it by meeting a certain academic requirement, such as GPA, test scores, a career goal, or through an essay competition. Your financial aid package may include both Need and Merit-based aid.

National Association of Intercollegiate Athletics (NAIA) The NAIA represents smaller schools and can provide scholarships.

National Merit Scholarship A distinction award you can receive if you score high enough on the NMSQT/PSAT (National Merit Scholar Qualifying Test/Preliminary Scholastic Aptitude Test). The test may be administered for practice during your sophomore year, but only your junior-year score counts.

National Collegiate Athletic Association (NCAA) The main association for intercollegiate athletics, the NCAA is made up of three divisions - I, II, and III. Division I and II offer track scholarships.

National Junior College Athletic Association (NJCAA) The association that overseas two-year programs. The NJCAA is divided into three divisions - I, II, and III. Divisions I and II offer track scholarships. See also Junior college.

NCAA Clearinghouse An organization established by the NCAA that determines if you are eligible for an official visit and to be recruited by NCAA D-I or D-II schools. You should register with the Clearinghouse at the start of your junior year of high school.

Need-Based Aid If the cost of attendance for your college exceeds your Expected Family Contribution (EFC), you will be eligible for need-based aid to cover the difference. You may be awarded a financial-aid package that consists of a combination of grants, scholarships, loans, and work-study. The total amount of your package will be determined by a combination of demonstrated financial need, federal award maximums, and your school's available funds.

Nonqualifier A nonqualifier cannot practice, compete or receive institutional financial aid for one academic year in Division I and II, and has three seasons of competition in Division I.

Official Visit Your trip to a college campus, paid in whole or in part by that institution. You are permitted by the NCAA to take one expense-paid visit to each of five different schools that are recruiting you during your senior year, regardless of how many sports you play. Visits are limited to 48 hours. You must pay for all additional visits.

Partial Qualifier You can receive a scholarship, practice, but not play games during your first year of school. If you are able to complete your academic degree in four years, you may stay at school a fifth year, giving you four years of eligibility.

Patriot League The NCAA D-I athletic conference that includes Bucknell, U.S. Military Academy, Lehigh, U.S. Naval Academy, American U., Lafayette, and Holy Cross, and does not offer track scholarships except for American.

Pell Grants Given by the Federal Government, these grants are awarded to those students demonstrating exceptional financial need. Pell grants do not need to be paid back.

Perkins Loans Awarded by each school, these low-interest loans (around 5%) are given to students who demonstrate exceptional financial need. Repayment of this loan begins nine months after you graduate, leave school, or drop to less than half-time student status.

Perkins & Stafford Loan Two types of need-based loans that are regularly included within a student's need-based financial aid package.

Personal Identification Number (PIN) When a student registers with the clearinghouse, he or she picks a four-digit PIN. This PIN will allow the student to check his or her eligibility online or by phone. For high schools, each school selects a five-digit PIN that allows high-school personnel to access specific information through the clearinghouse Web site.

The Parent Loans For Undergraduate Students (PLUS) And Supplemental Loans For Students (SLS) Two federal programs that assist families who don't qualify for need-based aid or who need help with their family contribution.

Private Counselors You may consult private counselors as you prepare to select and apply to colleges. They may operate as consultants or as employees of educational service providers such as Kaplan or the Princeton Review. Private counselors can help you assess your personality and academic needs to form a list of desirable college attributes. They can also help you figure out where and to how many schools you should apply. Private counselors can give you more attention than the average high school guidance counselor, but they can be pricey.

Profile The CSS/Financial Aid PROFILE is a customized financial aid application form required at certain colleges, which collects additional financial information to determine eligibility for institutional aid.

Proposition 48 This law states that a student athlete must meet certain requirements if he wants to practice and play during his freshman year at a NCAA Division I or Division II school.

Prospective Student Athlete Once you begin your freshmen year of high school, you may meet with college coaches but only if you initiate contact during an unofficial visit.

Preliminary Standard Aptitude Test (PSAT) The PSAT is administered by the college Board. You may take the PSAT in order to familiarize yourself with the test and kinds of questions you'll encounter on the SAT. The PSAT is also used as the qualifying test for the National Merit Scholar competition. This test is usually taken during your junior year of high school, but a practice PSAT may be given during your sophomore year. Like the SAT, the PSAT uses multiple-choice questions to test verbal and mathematical reasoning ability.

Qualifier A qualifier may practice, compete and receive institutional financial aid in his or her first year of enrollment at a Division I or II college.

Quiet period The college coach may not have any in-person contact with a student or the student's parents off the college campus. The coach may not watch the student play or visit the student's high school during this time. The student and his or her parents may visit a college campus during this time. A coach may write or telephone a student or his or her parents during this time.

Redshirt A term that describes you if you sit out a year of competition. If you are injured during your freshmen year or your college coach feels you need an extra year to develop, he may "redshirt" you. You would be permitted to practice with the team but not allowed to play in games. Redshirt athletes must complete their four years of athletic eligibility within six years.

SAT II The SAT II assesses knowledge in various subject areas. Most colleges require the writing test, a math test, and a foreign language test. They are taken in the spring of your junior year and the fall of your senior year. If the test is linked to a specific subject like chemistry, it's best to take the test as soon as possible upon the completion of the course.

Scholarship A type of financial aid that does not require repayment or employment and is usually awarded to students who demonstrate potential for academic or athletic achievement.

Scholastic Assessment Test (SAT) The SAT is administered by the College Board and is the most widely used college admissions test. The SAT uses multiple-choice questions to assess verbal and mathematical reasoning ability and an essay section. The SAT is taken during your junior and/or senior years. You may take this test multiple times if you wish to improve your score.

Sliding Scale A provision of the NCAA's Bylaw 14.3 that calculates minimum GPA and SAT/ACT scores in order for you to be an eligible recruit. The higher your GPA, the lower your SAT/ACT requirement, and visa-versa.

Sports Agent Someone who wants to handle all of your affairs (contract negotiation, sponsorships, financial planning, etc) should you make it to the pros. You are in violation of NCAA rules if you agree to let a sports agent represent you while you are still in high school or college.

Student-Expense Budget The total cost of attending a certain college for one academic year. Your financial need determined by the federal need analysis formula is the difference between the total cost of attending a college and your Family's Expected Contribution.

Student Release Form A document that you and your guidance counselor complete verifying your academic eligibility to compete at a NCAA D-I or D-II school.

Stafford Loans These loans, both subsidized (need based) and unsubsidized (non-need based), are guaranteed by the federal government and available to fund your education. Federal Stafford Loans are the most common source of education loan funds.

Student Aid Report (SAR) The official notification sent to you four to six weeks after filing the FAFSA. This report explains your FEC in relation to your school's expected cost of attendance. You may be required to submit this document to the financial aid office at the college you decide to attend.

Subsidized Loans Subsidized loans are based upon financial need. With these loans, the interest is paid by the federal government until the repayment period begins and during authorized periods of deferment afterwards.

Test Prep Preparing you for the college admissions tests is big business. There are books, videos, CD-ROMs, and classroom courses you can purchase designed to help you do your best on the tests. It is wise to do some prep for the test. At a minimum, look over the informational packet about each test to familiarize yourself with the number and type of questions you'll be expected to answer. And don't expect miracles - you'll have to do some hard work to make any kind of test prep successful.

Title IX Also referred to as gender equity, this law mandates that institutions that receive federal funding, among other things, are not allowed to discriminate on the basis of sex. This means that schools have had to increase funding and opportunities for women's athletics.

Transcript Your high school academic record. Your guidance counselor or registrar compiles this list of all your courses, grades, and standardized test scores. Your college will ask for official copies of your transcript. They should be signed across the seal by the appropriate school official and should not be opened.

Transfer Despite your best efforts, you may find that your chosen school isn't the perfect fit, or, you may start out at junior college and decide that it's time to attend a four-year University. In either case, you may need to transfer to a different school. Transferring can be a tricky process, especially when it comes time to figure out how many of your previously earned credits will count at your new school. To make your transition as simple as possible, request application materials from prospective schools as early as possible and figure out how your credits will be accounted for before you apply.

University Universities generally support both undergraduate and graduate programs and tend to be larger than colleges. You may find more research opportunities at a university, but you might get less attention from professors than at a college.

Unofficial Visit Any visit to a college campus by a student or his or her parents, paid for by the student or the student's parents. The only expense a student may receive is three complimentary admissions to a home contest.

Unsubsidized Loans Unsubsidized loans are not need-based; so all students are eligible to receive them. Interest payments begin immediately on unsubsidized loans, although you can waive the payments and the interest will be capitalized.

Verbal Commitment When a student verbally indicates that, he or she plans to attend a college or university and play college sports there. A verbal commitment is not binding for the college or the student.

Waiver A process to set aside NCAA rules because of specific, extraordinary circumstances that prevented a student from meeting the rules. A college on behalf of the student must file a waiver.

Walk-ons Usually unrecruited athletes who make the roster by proving themselves at open tryouts. This is difficult depending on the school. Some schools rely on walk ons to fill out their team while others discourage walk-ons. Make sure you would be comfortable attending the school if you do not end up competing for the team.

Weighted GPA Some high schools add 0.5 grade points to grades earned in AP or IB courses to reflect their unusual level of difficulty. If you have taken such courses, your GPA may be considered weighted. Some colleges convert weighted GPAs to standard GPAs for the purposes of comparison.

Work-study An institutionally or federally funded employment program that provides students with part-time jobs - generally 10 to 15 hours per week.

INTERNATIONAL STUDENTS

If you are an international student considering playing baseball at an American College or University, you are not alone. Thousands of international students pursue a college baseball experience each year within the United States.

If you are not a U.S. citizen and you are interested in playing baseball at the college level in the United States, then here is what you will need to do:

- With thousands of college programs to choose from, you will need to get help from a good advisor.

- If English is not your first language then you will need to take the TOEFL (Test of English as a Foreign Language) or provide evidence that you are proficient in English. Most colleges and universities differ on the score needed for acceptance into the school, but usually a score of 213 is suitable for the most prestigious schools in America.

- You may also need to take the SAT or ACT. Most colleges and universities ask to see both the SAT and TOEFL results of international student athletes.

- You should begin both the recruitment and application process more than a year in advance. The earlier you start talking with coaches and admissions officers the better your chances are of getting admitted and competing at the school of your choice.

- You will need to obtain an I-20 Certificate of Eligibility from the school you plan to attend and also an F-1.

10 THINGS TO REMEMBER DURING THE RECRUITING PROCESS

Though there are many ways to attract a college coach's attention, if you make use of the following ten suggestions, you will be ahead of your competition:

1. **Succeed In The Classroom.** You must achieve certain academic requirements to be eligible to play college baseball. Don't let poor grades limit your choices. Strive for excellence!

2. **Keep An Open Mind.** Even if you have your heart set on one college team, keep your options open with a wide range of schools on your Target List.

3. **Promote Yourself To College Coaches.** Don't wait for coaches to find you. Call, write, or email coaches to let them know that you want to play for their team.

4. **Use All Your Resources.** Get your parents, high school coach, summer league coach, and guidance counselor involved in the recruiting process.

5. **Improve Your Entire Package.** A good attitude, character, work ethic, and hustle are all important attributes that college coaches look for in players.

6. **Attend Showcases, Tournaments And Prospect Camps.** These events are perfect opportunities to demonstrate your ability to many college coaches and pro scouts. They also let you see how you stack up with other players in your area.

7. **Explore All Sources Of Financial Aid.** Many students receive other sources of financial aid, not just athletic scholarships.

8. **Learn About All Your Options.** Become familiar with the different divisions and keep an open mind. Visit different campuses, use the Internet to research college websites, and ask questions. Remember, you are not only choosing a place to compete athletically, but you are selecting a new home.

9. **Set Goals And Deadlines.** Make lists of academic and athletic accomplishments that you want to achieve during each year of high school.

10. **Have Fun.** Play for the love of the game.

HOW DID WE DO?

Thank you for purchasing our High School Athlete's Guide to College Baseball. Even though we are confident of our ability to help athletes like you navigate the recruiting process, we are always striving to improve. We would appreciate your input on what we can do to make this Guide more educational for future readers.

Your name (optional): _____

Your email address: _____

	Very	A Lot	Somewhat	Not Really	Not at all
How relevant was the Guide's information?	❏	❏	❏	❏	❏
How thorough was the Guide?	❏	❏	❏	❏	❏
How accurate was the Guide's information?	❏	❏	❏	❏	❏
How easy was the Guide to use?	❏	❏	❏	❏	❏
How appealing was the Guide's design?	❏	❏	❏	❏	❏

What overall grade would you give the Guide? (1-10, 10 being the best) _____

What were the Guide's strongest points? _____

How could the Guide be improved? _____

Was there anything not in the Guide that you wanted to know more about? _____

Would you recommend this book to other athletes?   ❏ Yes   ❏ No

Other Comments:
_____
_____

May we use your comments for promotional purposes?   ❏ Yes   ❏ No

Thank you for you help!
Please tear out this page and fax it to
914-244-0387 or mail it to:

College Bound Sports
364 Adams Street
Bedford Hills, NY 10507

Wayne Mazzoni
287 Courtland Ave.
Black Rock, CT 06605
203-260-4932   Wayne@WayneMazzoni.com
www.WayneMazzoni.com

Resources for high school and college baseball players.

www.ingramcontent.com/pod-product-compliance
Lightning Source LLC
Chambersburg PA
CBHW080737230426
43665CB00020B/2775